HAMMERIN' HANK!

By
DAN SCHLOSSBERG

STADIA SPORTS
PUBLISHING, INC.

HAMMERIN' HANK
The Henry Aaron Story

*To Samantha,
an All-Star
in any league*

April, 1974

Vol. 1. No. 1

SPORTSCOPE

Publisher
HY ROSS

Editor
ART PORETZ

Managing Editor
DON SMITH

Circulation Director
ALVIN SHAFKOWITZ

Advertising Manager
LON WEITZNER

STADIA SPORTS PUBLISHING, INC., 180 Madison Avenue, New York, N.Y. 10016

TABLE OF CONTENTS

FOREWORD

■ It wasn't easy to grow up in Passaic, New Jersey, and be a fan of the Milwaukee—or Atlanta—Braves, especially when all your friends rooted for the New York Yankees, New York Mets, or the transplanted Brooklyn Dodgers and New York Giants.

It was even harder growing up in New Jersey as a Hank Aaron fan. His name was never considered in baseball discussions, even after it became clear in the mid-1960's that he was destined to reach baseball heights never attained before.

In Passaic, which is less than a half-hour's drive from New York City, the kids talked about Mickey Mantle, Willie Mays, Duke Snider and lesser heroes who had the good fortune to wear Yankee pinstripes or other New York designation. The argument that Whitey Ford was better than Warren Spahn never did make much sense to me, and I really blew my cool when my friends started saying Roger Maris was a better rightfielder than Henry Aaron.

I can remember playing stickball in my backyard or at a friend's and pretending I was a different Brave every time I came to bat. My favorites, of course, were Hank Aaron and Eddie Mathews. History proved them to be the greatest home-run hitting pair of teammates who ever played, but it might still be difficult to convince New York fans that Mathews and Aaron were more productive than Ruth and Gehrig, Mantle and Maris, or Snider and Hodges.

Mathews was the man who made me a Braves' fan. It happened in 1957, when the only thing I knew about baseball was that I hated the Yankees. Who in his right mind likes a team that wins every year? It was a crashing bore to see the Yanks in the World Series and it was even worse to see them win it.

So, when Mathews made a dazzling grab of Bill Skowron's liner to end the seventh and deciding game of the 1957 Series—won by the Braves—I was hooked. There was at least one nine-year-old Milwaukee Braves fan in Passaic.

My love affair with the Braves—and with baseball—grew quickly. In 1959, when the Dodgers and Braves met in a best of three playoff to determine the National League's World Series representative, I had my heart set on watching Milwaukee win back the 1957 World Series crown which I felt was unfairly stolen by the Yankees in 1958.

Los Angeles won the first game, 3-2, and I still remember my great disappointment when Fred Haney, then the Milwaukee manager, started Carl Wiley in that game instead of one of his veteran stars. Haney let me down again in the second game when he lifted Lew Burdette in the ninth inning. The Braves entered the inning with a 5-2 lead but came out of it tied. I had been called away from the tube for supper when the bad news came. Felix Mantilla's error had let in a Dodger run in the 12th. The Braves lost, 6-5. It wasn't easy to face my friends in school after that.

Despite the post-season defeat, 1959 was a good year for the Braves. And it was the first year I really noticed Hank Aaron. He was 25 then—the same age as I am now—and I was 11. In addition to my 11th birthday party and a trip to Puerto Rico, the highlights of my year were Aaron's .355 batting average and the

Braves ruining Harvey Haddix' 12-inning perfect game.

By 1960, I was thoroughly hooked on Hank. To me, he was Mickey Mantle, Willie Mays, and Stan Musial all rolled up in one body. My devotion to him was so intense and so widely-known among my friends that they called me "Hank." Well, at least I got the other kids to realize who he was.

I finally met Hank for the first time in 1965, when I was a senior at Passaic High and he was in his last year as a Milwaukee Brave. I had arranged for Bobby Bragan, then the Milwaukee manager, to write an article on sportsmanship for The Jersey Key, the publication of the Key Clubs of New Jersey, and I had asked the New York Mets' publicity department if I could meet Bragan when the Braves came to town. I still remember the date: May 9, 1965.

In addition to editing The Jersey Key, I was also sports editor of The Hilltop Star, my high school paper, and the meeting with Bragan at Shea Stadium provided a fine story for that publication. It was a great day in my life.

Later that year, I found myself at Syracuse University, where I realized I could tie my twin interests in baseball and journalism together and become a professional sportswriter. I did play-by-play baseball for the Syracuse ball team, covered the team for the Daily Orange, and even wrote pre-season predictions of the major league races. In addition, radio reception was excellent in that upstate New York community, and I was able to pick up Braves' broadcasts from Atlanta on WSB. In the New York area, WABC is too close to allow good reception of the Atlanta station, but Syracuse is some 250 miles from New York City and WABC is just another strong-but-distant station.

By the time I reached my senior year in September 1968, I had spent three college summers as a reporter on the real-life Passaic Herald-News, where one of my assignments included an interview with Satchel Paige, then on the active roster of the Braves so that he could qualify for the baseball pension plan. That interview, again at Shea Stadium, gave me another chance to see Hank Aaron close up and to give him a quick hello. Then, as now, I held him in awe.

Shortly before graduation, I made a weekend visit to Montreal to see the Braves and Aaron. I was putting together a sports show for WAER, the Syracuse campus station, and it included an interview with Aaron. I found him to be very friendly, polite and cooperative, although I had to get up my nerve before I even approached him. The fine interview Aaron gave me "made" my weekend ... even though the weather was terrible.

By May 21, my classes were over and I was set to return to Passaic, where the Herald-News had offered me a full-time job as a combination news and sports reporter. That night—I was prepared to leave Syracuse for good the next day—I got a call from The Associated Press office in Newark, New Jersey.

"How would you like to be the AP Sports Editor for New Jersey?" asked a strange voice. I didn't have to answer and I couldn't if I had wanted to. I was too shocked.

I started at the AP in July. I had made it. I was a professional sports reporter. Of course, the AP job required lots of newswriting and reporting, and I doubled as Broadcast Editor for a while, but my main job—in my mind, at least—was sports. Unfortunately, though, New Jersey had every sport but the one I liked the most—baseball. If I wanted to write about that sport, I knew I would have to look elsewhere—and I did.

I wrote letters to the editors of the 30-odd pre-season baseball magazines, asking if I could contribute to them. Only one—Alan Goldfarb, then the editor of Complete Sports Publications of Brooklyn—gave a positive reply. "Let's meet in Madison Square Garden for lunch and talk it over," he said.

We met, he quizzed me, and then asked if I'd like to write his team preview sections in BASEBALL ILLUSTRATED magazine the following spring. I jumped at the chance. That lucky break opened the door wide, and I've been writing for all sorts of sports books and magazines since—and loving every minute of it.

I've not only interviewed Hank Aaron—and all the Braves—any number of times, but have also religiously kept baseball scrapbooks containing news-worthy items dating back to the early 1960s. A photograph I took of Aaron and Mathews in the colorful new Braves' uniforms in March 1973 is now in the baseball Hall of Fame in Cooperstown, and I take great delight in kidding some of the younger Braves that I'm in the Hall.

Any Braves fan wants his team to win—just as I do—but when the team loses, there is still the prospect of avoiding a "total loss" if Hank Aaron hits a home run. I always harbor that hope, even if the Braves are down, 10-0, in the ninth inning.

I really haven't changed my outlook on life or view of sports. I like to swim and play tennis and—believe it or not—stickball, and I don't like to watch or listen to any other sport than baseball. I would rather hear a game between the Texas Rangers and Cleveland Indians than watch the Super Bowl on television. The biggest news of the winter months, for me, is not the progress of the hockey or basketball teams, but the trades made by the baseball teams.

This book is really an account of my love affair with Hank Aaron and the Braves. It is written not only from a sportswriter's point of view, but also from a fan's.

When I told my friends 10 years ago that Hank Aaron would break Babe Ruth's record, they laughed. "Don't be ridiculous," they said. But I wasn't, was I?

DAN SCHLOSSBERG
Passaic, New Jersey

Babe Ruth (L), the pursued, and Atlanta's Hank Aaron, the pursuer.

THE FINAL ASSAULT

■ "One ties, two tops."

The scoreboard behind the left-centerfield fence flashed the message in huge electric letters as more than 40,000 fans filed out of Atlanta Stadium after the last out of the 1973 baseball season had been recorded.

Henry Louis Aaron, Atlanta Braves outfielder, had ended that memorable season just one home run away from a career total of 714, the same number collected by the legendary Babe Ruth.

Though he had one of his most remarkable campaigns at age 39 in 1973, Hank Aaron did not equal Ruth's record. Barring some unforeseen catastrophe, he will not only equal but far surpass it early in the 1974 season, then throw down his gauntlet as if daring some future slugger to challenge the new mark.

"We open up in San *Francisco and I haven't hit a home run there in about three years," Aaron said, referring to the Braves' three-game opening series of the 1974 campaign. "My chances of hitting a home run there don't look too good.

"I'll probably play all three games out there, but I'm hoping I can hit it here in Atlanta, although I'll do the best I can regardless of where I play."

Says manager Eddie Mathews:

"We open in San Francisco next season, and I think what we'll do is play Henry in the first game there, then sit him down and play him in our home opener. I think we owe that much to the Atlanta fans.

"This is giving both places a fair shake. We owe it to the Giants to at least have their fans see Aaron on opening day. Then we'll rest him up for the flight back across the country, which we normally would do anyway. If we get lucky, he could tie it in San Francisco and break it in

Atlanta. If he hits two the first day, well, that's life. I'll tell you one thing, when Henry plays, he plays 100 per cent.

"I don't know where Hank Aaron will break Ruth's record, but I can tell you one thing. Ten years from the day he hits it, three million people will say they were there."

Aaron's greatest home run day came in San Francisco on June 21, 1959, when he hit three in one game, but that was before the Giants moved from Seals Stadium, originally a minor league park, to Candlestick Park in 1960.

There are many reasons why the tying and record-breaking home runs would be more spectacular if they came in Atlanta. First, the opening night of the 1974 season will be dedicated to Aaron, marking the highlight of a Chamber of Commerce program called "Atlanta Salutes Hank Aaron." Donations to a Hank Aaron scholarship drive will be announced and special bumperstickers will be distributed.

Second, a massive fireworks display will commemorate the big home runs with a bang. "It will be something people will remember," insists the man in charge, Jerry Broad of the

* At press time NL schedule was uncertain because of San Diego franchise situation.

9

I was there when Hank Aaron hit his 715th
career home run to pass Babe Ruth as the top
home run hitter in the history of Baseball.

Date _____

Place _____

715

Braves will present this certificate to Atlanta fans who witness Hank's 715th HR.

Nationwide Fireworks Co. of Saginaw, Mich.

In addition, the Braves' public relations department has printed more than 35,000 "I Was There" certificates for both the 714th and 715th home runs, hoping to distribute them to fans who witness the historic homers. All those not distributed will be destroyed.

Aaron himself would prefer to hit his record-tying and record-breaking homers at home because he feels he owes a debt of gratitude to Atlanta fans.

After hitting a home run in the 1972 All-Star Game in Atlanta, Aaron observed, "That homer is the most dramatic I've ever hit. It had

to be for a couple of reasons. First of all, I have not had good luck in All-Star Games and second, there are the fans.

"You can talk about the fans, but the people in Atlanta have been great to me. They came to see me hit one and I was pleased to come through. If I had to have a good All-Star Game, I'm glad it came here in Atlanta."

Aaron's pursuit of Ruth's record has produced some negative fan reaction, however. Early in the 1973 season, he received a torrent of hate mail, apparently generated by the fact that Hank, who is black, dared to challenge the record of Ruth, who is still regarded by some as a symbol of white supremacy.

"You have to be concerned," said Braves' traveling secretary Don Davidson, who ordered special security for Aaron on all Atlanta road trips. "There are a lot of crazy people around. We've proved that in this country."

Stickers reading "AARON IS RUTHLESS" sprouted on some car bumpers. Letters came in asking Hank not to challenge the record. "Do they want me to stop hitting home runs?" he asked. "Don't they realize I'm just doing my job?"

Aaron did not stop. In fact, he accelerated his pace in 1973, powering 40 home runs in just 392 times at bat, or 10.2 home runs per 100 times at bat, a pace exceeded only six times in baseball history (by Babe Ruth three times and by Mickey Mantle, Hank Greenberg and Roger Maris once each).

"For every letter I get against setting the record," said Aaron, "I get about four or five for it. Nowadays, I think most people want to see all records erased. It shows a profession in sports, an attitude that we can do better now than athletes did in the past."

Aaron, who has often claimed he needed incentive to chase Ruth's mark, has several as he takes the final stages of his race into the 1974 season.

Since he has promised to retire at the end of the season, he has only one more chance to get into the World Series, which he last played in following the 1958 National League campaign. A good performance by Hank in 1974 could go a long way toward making the Braves a contending team, particularly if the pitching staff improves.

Also, Aaron wants to hit as many home runs as he can to set a standard that can never be equalled. Of the players currently active, Johnny Bench is given the best chance of ever reaching 714, but he would have to hit nearly 36 a year for the next 15 seasons to do it. Since he is a catcher, his career is unlikely to last that long unless he changes positions.

Finally the great Atlanta star wants to repudiate the bigots who appealed to their base instincts in writing hate letters.

"I am better when the pressure is on and there is motivation," he says. "Breaking Ruth's record is motivation. I am happy to be in a position where I can break it.

"I'm the type of person

who needs something to shoot for—a goal—and when I have one, the juices start flowing. That's why I think the pressure helps me. I need to have an overwhelming responsibility that will keep me in the lineup as often as possible. Lots of things motivate a player, but nothing does it like the chance for a championship."

"I've always looked at baseball as a job. I go out there and do a job, and do what is expected of me and perhaps don't show a lot of emotion about it."

But, inside, Hank Aaron cares. He plays handball and swims in the winter months to keep his trim 6-0, 185-pound figure, and reports to the Braves' spring training camp in better condition than most of his younger teammates. He is always within five or six pounds of his playing weight when he checks in.

It is a matter of pride with Hank that he be ready to play when the season opens each April. He has always said that his health is the one factor which could halt his race with Ruth.

"I won't punish myself to go after Ruth's record—not physically or mentally," he admitted during a rare mid-season slump in 1972.

"For instance, I would never let my personal ambition to go after another man's record cause me to lose the respect of the fans and the press. I couldn't stand to hear them say I was hurting the team by hanging around just going after the record."

That was the accusation leveled against him in May 1973, when he had 10 home runs and a .240 average. But Aaron insists he was not in shape at the end of spring training—though he thought he was—and blames that factor for his low average.

"People said I was selfish and going for home runs, which was untrue," Aaron recalls. "I felt I was in shape, but I wasn't in top condition when we broke spring camp. About the middle of the season, my legs got stronger and I felt a lot better."

Something happened to Hank between the opening of the season and the All-Star Game at Kansas City July 24. His first half and second half were like two different seasons. After the All-Star Game, he hit .398 for the rest of the year to finish at .301, the 14th time he has topped .300.

His achievement is all the more amazing because it was achieved in the brightest glare of publicity ever accorded a sports figure. As

Hank Greenberg is one of six men who exceeded Aaron's seasonal HR ratio.

Aaron approached Ruth's record, writers and broadcasters from all corners of America—and even foreign reporters from Mexico, England and Japan—converged on the Braves. Since the team seemed certain to wind up fifth in the six-team Western Division of the National League, the only story was Aaron.

Atlanta publicity director Bob Hope, who had his hands full coping with the deluge of journalists, was forced to set up a special news conference room adjacent to the Braves' clubhouse for post-game interviews with Aaron.

"The newsmen don't bother me, I'm much more worried about the pitchers who are trying to prevent me from breaking Ruth's record than I am about the people who are going to write and talk about it."

Despite his disclaimer Aaron occasionally showed signs of stress during the 1973 campaign and might have retired after the season had he passed Ruth.

During spring training at West Palm Beach, Florida, Aaron told a local newspaper reporter: "If I should get extra lucky and hit forty-two homers this season, I'm planning on quitting. But my real plan, which is more realistic, is to hit at least forty-two in two seasons."

Late in the campaign, he confided, "It's been a tiresome thing, constantly talking about Babe Ruth. I just want to hurry up and get it over with. I can't recall a day this year or the last part of last year when I did not hear the name Babe Ruth. Certainly, I would like to get it over with, but I'm not going to go up there and press for home runs.

"I used to love to come to the ballpark. Now I hate it. Every day becomes a little tougher because of all this. Writers, tape recorders, microphones, cameras, questions and more questions. Roger Maris lost his hair the season he hit sixty-one. I still have all my hair, but when it's over, I'm going home to Mobile and fish for a long time."

Aaron did take that long-awaited fishing trip in his 27-foot yacht Dorinda after the 1973 season ended, but the questions started again when the Braves opened their 1974 spring training camp.

Asked by one reporter to put himself in a writer's shoes and ask himself a question that had not been asked before, Hank responded, "I can't think of a one."

The year 1974 marks the third and final year of Aaron's $200,000-per-season contract, which he insists will be the last he will have as an active player.

"I'm not interested in playing after 1974," he said. "I want to see my kids grow up. Also, I don't really know of anything else I could do in the game. I'm certainly not going to catch Ty Cobb in hits. He had way too many."

Aaron does, however, have some goals other than home runs. One big milestone would be the all-time record for runs batted in, currently held by none other than Babe Ruth.

By knocking in 77 runs in 1974 (he had 96 RBI in 1973), Hank will become the all-time RBI king. The Braves' star can also move into first place—ahead of Ty Cobb—if he plays 70 games and bats 142 times this season. He will take third place—behind Cobb and Stan Musial—in hits when he records his seventh safety of the new season. Should Aaron produce 122 hits (he had 118 in 1973) he will rank second on the career list, with only Cobb ahead of him.

Aaron probably won't even think about these objectives until the race with Ruth is over. Perhaps the pressure won't stop at 715. Will the media pursue Aaron even after he has passed sports' greatest milestone? The question is academic, but it won't bother Henry one way or the other. He plans to keep right on going past the mark and predicts he'll wind up with about 735 lifetime home runs.

"I know that's only 22 in 1974, but that's a lot for a 40-year-old man," he says. He celebrated his 40th birthday on Feb. 5.

A study in modesty, Aaron had predicted only 30 to 35 homers for himself in 1973.

"I said at the beginning of last season that if I could hit forty home runs or thereabouts, I would be in great shape," he recalls. "I felt that, at the beginning of the season, I would hit thirty to thirty-five home runs.

"Going into the 1974 season, I have hopes of having the same type of year I had in 1973."

Babe Ruth hit just 22 homers at age 39 and only six at age 40, when he retired as an active player. Aaron far exceeded Babe's performance as a 39-year-old

Ex-Dodger Claude Osteen has served up 13 career gopher balls to Aaron.

L-R: Aaron, Dave Johnson, Darrell Evans. All topped 40-homer plateau in 1973.

and is virtually certain to out-perform him at age 40 as well.

Aaron has his sights set out on the 1974 campaign and the milestone shots which are certain to come during the season's first month. He's even predicting that he will hit the big home runs against veteran pit-chers whom he has faced before.

"The pitcher will have to be somebody with guts enough to challenge me with his best pitch," says Aaron, an All-Star for 19 straight seasons and the game's most respected hitter. "It won't be a rookie and it won't be a border-liner. It will be somebody like Seaver, Gib-son, or Carlton—somebody

not afraid to throw his best pitch."

Among active pitchers, lefthander Claude Osteen has thrown Aaron more gopher balls than anyone else—13. The all-time leader, righthander Don Drysdale, gave up 17 of Aaron's 713.

"I would be very nervous if I were facing Hank when he was going for his record home run," admits Osteen, who has always given the Braves trouble despite Aaron's heroics. "One of the reasons I've given more homers to Aaron than anyone except Don Drysdale is that I've been pitching quite a few years. As Henry himself says, 'He (Osteen) faces us four times a year, it stands to reason he's given up the most homers.' "

According to former pitcher Ernie Johnson, now an announcer for the Braves, Aaron's secret is his low-key approach, coupled with a fine memory. The slugger keeps a mental book on all pitchers he faces.

"Henry Aaron is simply smarter than all the pitchers," claims the lanky broadcaster. "He deceives pitchers. One of his secrets is his slow manner. He puts pitchers to sleep."

Aaron explains his own batting philosophy. "The pitcher has got only a ball. I've got a bat. The percentage of weapons is in my favor."

Aaron's home park— Atlanta Stadium—also is a great help to anyone who thrives on the long ball. Pitchers refer to it sarcastically as "the Launching Pad" because the thin air in the Georgia capital enables balls to zoom out of the batter's box as if they were launched by a bazooka. Three Braves, Aaron, Dave Johnson and Darrell Evans, hit 40 or more homers in 1973 to make Atlanta the first team in baseball history to boast three 40-homer men in the same season.

Twenty-six of Aaron's home runs came in Atlanta Stadium, and the stadium's friendly power alleys have contributed heavily to his average of 40 homers a year since the Braves fled Milwaukee following the 1965 season. He's hit 179 in the Georgia ballpark in his eight seasons there. Most remarkable, perhaps, is that since his 34th birthday, Aaron has hit 29, 44, 38, 47, 34, and 40 home runs per season, a spectacular power output for a man supposed to be in the twilight of his career.

His total of 74 over the 1972 and 1973 seasons was achieved without the advantage of batting against the Braves' pitching staff, worst in the league by a wide margin both years. Though the team led the National League in all offensive categories, the Braves' inexperienced pitchers constantly blew leads in the late innings.

No one could blame Aaron for the team's lackluster showing. In addition to his solid performance at the plate, he responded well to his return to the outfield after two years at first base. His fielding, especially after the All-Star break, was outstanding.

"I've lost a step or two in the outfield," he admits, "but I get it back in knowing how to play the hitters."

Hank's throwing arm not

being what it once was, manager Eddie Mathews shifted Aaron from his familiar rightfield post to left.

"I moved Henry to the left simply because he doesn't have the long throwing arm anymore, and throws from left are easier," explained Mathews, who is co-holder with Aaron of the record for most home runs by team-mates (863). "It may be a coincidence, but as soon as he moved to left, he began hitting better."

Aaron had spent most of the 1971 and 1972 seasons at first base, a position he disliked and never really mastered defensively. He initially made the move in mid-1971 when Orlando Cepeda, the regular there, got hurt.

"I almost got killed a couple of times at first," Aaron said after learning he would return to the outfield in 1973. "I'd just as soon go back. I don't think playing first base saved that much wear and tear on me anyhow."

Plans for 1974 also call for Aaron to be in left field when he plays. The Hammer got into just 120 games in 1973, including several as a pinch-hitter, and may play even less in his final season.

"I leave it up to Henry every game," says Mathews.

"I check with him before I make out the lineup. If he wants to play, he's in. If he doesn't, that's his decision."

As a rule, Aaron sits out day games after night games and plays only one game of double-headers. He stuck rigidly to that schedule in 1973, even though there were times when he felt like swinging the bat. He explained that he did not want to tire himself out, as he had in 1972.

"I might have hit another home run here or there," he says, "but I could also have gone up with the bases loaded and not come through—costing us a ball game. Maybe somebody else—young and not as tired—could have gone up and done the job. I can't let one hit that means something to Hank Aaron get in the way of the ball club. I know I disappointed some fans, but the name of the game is still to win."

The importance of a well-rested Aaron is underlined by Mathews. "The pitchers are trying harder when Henry comes up," the manager observes. "They're not pitching around him, but seem to be putting a little extra on the ball. No one wants to be the guy who throws **the** ball as he gets closer."

Ex-Astro Jerry Reuss was out-guessed by Aaron when Hank hit 713th homer.

Aaron is still a guess hitter, just as he was when he came to his first spring training camp as a non-roster player with the 1954 Milwaukee Braves. "Guessing what the pitcher is going to throw is eighty per cent of being a successful hitter," Aaron insists when asked the wisdom of playing a hunch in the hitter's box. "The other twenty per cent is just execution."

After Hank powered a Jerry Reuss curve ball over the left-centerfield fence for home run No. 713 in Atlanta last Sept. 29, he admitted he had guessed correctly on the pitch. "He had walked me on two or three slow curves the previous time up, and I was just hoping he would throw it to me again," Aaron said.

Eddie Mathews marvels at the man. "His swing is just as smooth and effective today as it ever was," the manager says of his one-time teammate. "He never slows down. He does the job exactly as he has since coming to the Braves."

Babe Ruth might not think too highly of his record being challenged, according to one of his old teammates, but the challenger is a worthy successor, according to another.

Ruth's one-time roommate and card partner, Jimmy Reese, said of Aaron's challenge, "The Babe wouldn't have liked this. He always thought **he** was the best home run hitter. If he had known someone was going to break his record of 60 in one season, he would have hit 70. If he had known someone was going to hit 714, he would have hit 800."

Leo Durocher, veteran major league manager who also played with Ruth, sized up Hank in one short sentence. "Aaron is the best righthand hitter in baseball since Rogers Hornsby, period."

Durocher added, however, that he had never seen a man

Leo Durocher calls Hank "best right-handed hitter since Hornsby."

Aaron knows Ruth's home runs will always be legend simply because the man was bigger-than-life. Ruth was flamboyant, charismatic. Aaron is conservative and quiet.

"If I hit 750, it will just mean that Hank Aaron hit 750 home runs, that's all," he says. "Ruth's homers are always going to be legend. Somebody can come along and hit 800 home runs and it's never going to mean as much as Babe Ruth's record."

Perhaps it was the glory of Ruth's achievement which prompted the noted astrologer, Jeanne Dixon, to predict in 1971 that Aaron would not surpass it. "Yeah," said Lee Walburn, then the Braves' publicity director, "but she doesn't have to pitch against him."

Although he is a modest man, Aaron is proud of his baseball skills. "I never said I was a Willie Mays in the outfield and I never claimed my arm was like Roberto Clemente's, but I've won a few Gold Gloves of my own," says the man who spent most of his career in an obscurity created by his own consistency. "I was proud that whenever I fielded a base hit, it got back to the right base so it could be handled. I don't recall having a bad year. My

who could hit the ball as far as Babe Ruth.

The Ruth-Aaron comparison is a story in itself. The game has changed in many ways in the 39 years since Ruth's retirement in 1935. For one thing, pitching has improved so much that the over-all major league batting average is now .252, down 30 points from a high of .282 in Ruth's era.

"I have no intention of making people forget Babe Ruth," Aaron mused late in the 1973 season. "I just want to make sure that they remember Hank Aaron. I hope I can inspire a few kids to be a success in life. I want to break Ruth's record as an example to children, especially black children."

best year for hitting the ball was 1959, when I hit .355. For a long time I was over .400, then I sprained my ankle running after a fly ball at Connie Mack Stadium in Philadelphia."

If consistency is the name of the game, Aaron has most certainly achieved it. Since his rookie year of 1954, he has never hit less than .265 or had less than 24 homers and 77 runs batted in. He's led the NL in every major hitting category—batting average, home runs, and runs batted in—at least twice, and taking his best output in each, can show the .355 average, 47 home runs (1971), and 132 runs batted in (1957). He was named the NL's Most Valuable Player in 1957 and The Sporting News' Player of the Year in 1956 and 1963.

It is quite likely he will far exceed his career lows in all departments in 1974 because he has one remaining personal ambition: to keep the home run record he sets. A 1974 campaign like the one in 1973 would give the slugger nearly 750 lifetime home runs.

"I don't think anyone else will ever get close to it," he says, explaining his wish for one last big season. "The pitching today is very difficult and the kids coming into baseball don't want to stay more than seven or eight years. They want to get out and try something else. That's okay, except that it takes longer than seven or eight years to hit more home runs than Babe Ruth."

When Hank retires after the 1974 season, it will be hard for baseball and the Braves to fill the void. And it will be hard for Aaron to hang up his spikes. Once baseball is in the bloodstream, it doesn't leave. For evidence, look at the list of old stars who hung on after they should have retired: Willie Mays, Warren Spahn, Mickey Mantle and Hoyt Wilhelm, among others. Hank Aaron does not want to be remembered that way.

"I'd like to bow out of the game as gracefully as possible," he confides. "I've stayed in the game to prove to myself that I could do certain things. But I'll get out for some young kid coming up. I wouldn't want to stand in his way.

"God has been good to me. Otherwise, I wouldn't be this close to breaking Ruth's record. If I do break it, great. It will be a dream come true. If I don't, I can say I gave it my best shot. I can say I didn't abuse my God-given talent." ●

ON THE THRESHOLD

■ As the Atlanta Braves entered their final week of the 1973 season, Hank Aaron had 39 home runs. He needed two to tie Babe Ruth's record and had five games in which to get them. All five games were scheduled to be played in Atlanta Stadium, Aaron's home park. The Los Angeles Dodgers would play three games there, the Houston Astros two. With the western division championship already clinched by Cin- cinnati, the only unfinished business in the division was Hank Aaron's race with Ruth.

TUESDAY, SEPTEMBER 25

As the Braves prepared for the first game against Los Angeles, several Dodger pitchers talked about testing their skills against Aaron's. "I wouldn't lay it in there for my own brother if he needed just one to beat Ruth's record," said ace righthander Don Sutton, who

Atlanta Stadium, the scene of Aaron's dramatic 1973 bid to overhaul Ruth.

would open the series for Los Angeles. "The thing that's bad for us pitchers is you don't have to lay it in there for him. Look at the chart—those are not Double-A pitchers he nails.

"Every time I face him, I throw something to diddle around and maybe get him to swing. I try to mess with his mind as much as I can because he sure tries to mess mine up. Like during batting practice, he might look over at me, grinning, and lick his fingers, stuff like that. Hank is a great needler."

Andy Messersmith, who one week earlier had thrown the pitch that enabled Atlanta's Dave Johnson to set a new home run mark for second basemen (43), added, "Yeah, I'd like to be out there when Aaron goes for the record. I think it would be exciting."

It was the Dodger tandem of Don Drysdale and Sandy Koufax who pinned the monicker "Bad Henry" on Aaron, not because he was bad, but because of the pain he inflicted on pitchers with such consistency. In addition to 17 career homers off Drysdale, Hank swatted seven off Koufax, proving the great lefthander threw occasional gopher balls between aspirin tablets.

In 1973, however, Aaron had managed only two

homers against Los Angeles, both off lefthander Al Downing—one at home and one on the road—as the Braves dropped 13 of their first 15 games with the Dodgers.

Sutton opened the series against Atlanta ace Phil Niekro, winless since August 15 though he had pitched well. Sutton scattered four hits—none by Aaron—as the Dodgers scored three off relief pitcher Dave Cheadle in the ninth to wrap up a 5-1 victory.

Aaron, saddled with an 0-for-4 collar, narrowly missed a home run in the late innings when he hit a long drive to Willie Davis in dead center. "But I knew it was an out when I hit it," he said later. "When you've hit 712, you know when the ball is likely to go out of the park."

WEDNESDAY, SEPTEMBER 26

It was a hot, muggy night and there was some question as to whether or not the game should be played. There was water in the outfield and the weatherman was calling for more rain. Yet, the game went ahead as scheduled, with Hank Aaron in the lineup. He got one hit, good for two runs batted in, in four at-bats. The Braves

lost, 9-8, when their bullpen failed to hold an 8-6 Atlanta lead in the ninth inning.

"I had a couple of good pitches to hit at tonight," said Aaron in the post-game news conference. "One in particular from Eddie Solomon after the back-to-back home runs by (Mike) Lum and (Darrell) Evans. It was right down the middle, but I was looking for a curve ball."

Aaron's infield pop-up had ended the game.

THURSDAY, SEPTEMBER 27

Hank Aaron felt good before the Thursday game, especially when he learned Claude Osteen was going to pitch. Osteen had been tough on him in recent seasons, but still remained first among active pitchers in yielding 13 Aaron home runs.

The slugger was loose and ready to challenge fate that night, but fate decided to play a cruel trick on him.

As the lineups were being announced for the 7:05 p.m. game, a hard downpour started. The field was already drenched from a steady all-day rain which had soaked the Greater Atlanta area. If the game were cancelled, there would be no chance to make it up because the Dodgers had a Friday night

Don Sutton admits that he tries to "psych" Aaron in head-to-head duels.

game in San Diego. Both Atlanta and Los Angeles had games scheduled for Saturday and Sunday, the last two days of the regular season.

Ordinarily, the umpires would have called the game without any question. Neither the Braves nor the Dodgers could alter their position in the standings. The game was virtually meaningless and playing under bad conditions could cause injuries. Yet, for the sake of one man and his pursuit of a record, the umpires delayed their decision.

Bill Bartholomay, Braves' chairman of the board, approached Aaron in the clubhouse. "If we play, will you play?" he asked. Hank answered, "I'll play, but that shouldn't be the deciding factor. Either the field is playable or it isn't. It's not a matter of personal records. It's a matter of 18 players. The outfield isn't in good shape. There can be a lot of pulled muscles out there."

Finally, umpire Tom Gorman made his decision. No game.

"When a game is rained out like this," reflected Henry as he peeled off his uniform, "especially in a park where you're comfortable, where you know you can hit home runs, it hurts."

But Braves' manager Eddie Mathews had intended to lift Aaron anyhow. "There was no way I was going to tell Hank to go out there and hit a home run under those conditions," he said. "I just wasn't going to play him, that's all. The field was brutal. It wasn't fair to Hank. It wasn't fair to the rest of the guys, either."

Before the game was called, Dodger broadcaster Vin Scully remarked, "Aaron has hit more homers than anyone alive. Now the Braves are going to see if he can walk on water." But it never came to that.

Even with a rainout, Aaron was the target of newsmen in the clubhouse. As other players quietly dressed and left, the home run star,

Tiny sparrow perches on Aaron's hand during final-week rainout in Atlanta.

dressed in a blue-and-gray baseball sweatshirt and long white underwear, sat on a stool in front of his locker and talked to the press. Two local writers, Jesse Outlar and Wayne Minshew of the Atlanta Constitution, sat alone with Aaron for a few minutes before a mob of reporters, broadcasters and photographers descended on the scene. As always, Hank didn't get excited, he patiently answered questions in a low voice.

There was a moment of silence as the group paused between questions to think up new angles for Aaron. Cameras clicked and TV film whirred as he sat there, waiting to field the next query as if he were in left field, waiting for the ball to be hit his way.

Suddenly, Furman Bisher, sports editor of the Atlanta Journal and a man who knows Aaron well, pushed through the edge of the mob scene. "Somebody say something," he demanded with a smile. "This is boring as hell!"

The questions started coming again, just as they had all season. Aaron knew that he had only two more days to go through the interview sessions before the arrival of the off-season and five months of well-deserved rest.

Gov. Jimmy Carter of Georgia, whose statehouse is less than a mile from Atlanta Stadium, made his way through the crowd of newsmen to introduce Gov. Sherman Tribbett of Delaware to Aaron. "He came all the way down here just to see you play," Carter told the veteran outfielder. "And it had to rain!"

Aaron didn't have to be reminded. He had two games left to hit three homers.

FRIDAY, SEPTEMBER 28

The Braves had no game slated for Friday. The hot, muggy weather continued in the Atlanta area while Aaron and the journalists sent to cover him enjoyed the luxury of forgetting baseball for a day. Hank spent the time with his family, taking a one-day respite from his relentless pursuit of Babe Ruth's record.

SATURDAY, SEPTEMBER 29

Leo Durocher's Houston Astros were in town for the beginning of a two-game series. Two lefthanders, Jerry Reuss and Dave Roberts, were named to pitch for the Astros. Both had been Aaron home run victims in 1973, Roberts only one week before in the Astrodome. Aaron also hit an Astrodome homer off Reuss on May 16.

The day began for Hank Aaron with a telegram from U.S. Senator Herman Talmadge (D-Ga.). It read: "Good hitting this weekend against the Astros. You have already gone down in baseball history as one of the greats of the game, and now you are on the brink of one of the most important moments in sports history. Our hopes are with you all the way to a new record."

Aaron, asked by a reporter if he could hit three homers for a new record, gave a realistic answer: "Oh, I can do it, I've done it before. It's just that it isn't likely."

There was an air of anticipation around Atlanta Stadium all day Saturday. A man walked up to the Braves' Advance Ticket Window and asked "Is Hank Aaron gonna play tonight?" It was a question repeated countless times that afternoon. A bigger question, perhaps, was: would the Braves play? The weather was again questionable, with showers predicted for the evening hours. Game time was 7:05.

The press, the fans, and Aaron himself were wondering what lay ahead. Could Hank hit one, two, or even three home runs in the next two games, or would he have to wait for 1974?

Just before game time, the electricity built up in the stands at Atlanta Stadium— and in the gathering thunderheads above. Some 17,000-plus fans stirred about as if they expected the imminent delivery of a first baby. Hot-dog wrappers swirled in a slight breeze near the leftfield foul pole. The scoreboard operator tried his hand at an Aaron message: "713" went up in huge electric numbers.

Braves' starter Carl Morton retired the Astros in the top of the first inning. Jerry Reuss took the mound for Houston in the bottom half. Mike Lum, playing Aaron's old position in rightfield, slammed a long double to right-center. Darrell Evans, like Lum a lefthand batter facing a lefthand pitcher, followed with his 41st home run of the year, far over the right-centerfield fence. The Braves led, 2-0, but the fans didn't care about that. All they knew was that Hank Aaron was coming to bat.

Even before the cheers for Evans had subsided, an even louder roar engulfed the stadium. No. 44 ambled toward the plate, slowly putting his batting helmet on, and made himself comfortable in the batter's box. He picked out a choice Reuss pitch and poked a single to left, disappointing the fans. But they were to get their money's worth later.

In the sixth, Lum and Evans hit back-to-back singles ahead of Aaron. The crowd quivered with ex-

pectancy as Hank approached the plate. Would The Hammer pick this dramatic spot to hit No. 713 and insure victory for the Braves? The fans did not have to wait long to find out. Reuss threw Aaron a slow curve ball. The righthanded batter snapped his wrists, flexed his powerful shoulder muscles, and powered the ball deep over the left-centerfield fence, well over 400 feet away. The big "713" was on the scoreboard before Aaron rounded third on his way home.

Atlanta Stadium rocked with applause as if the Braves had just won the World Series. The fans cheered on their feet, standing even after Aaron had disappeared into the dugout with the two teammates who had scored ahead of him. They kept up their lusty enthusiasm until Hank, coaxed by his teammates, emerged from the dugout to thank the crowd. This gesture prompted even louder applause for several moments before the game could be continued.

Dusty Baker followed Aaron's clout with another long home run, perhaps depriving Dave Johnson, the No. 5 batter, from a shot at the league's home run crown. Johnson, with 43 home runs for the season, trailed Pittsburgh's Willie Stargell by one, but had the misfortune to come up in the Saturday night game after successive home runs. He never saw a pitch he could hit. Reuss plunked him in the middle of the back with his first pitch, prompting a warning to both managers from plate umpire Dave Davidson and an automatic $50 fine for Reuss.

The home run by Aaron gave the Braves their third 40-homer man of 1973, a baseball record. But it frustrated fans who had crowded into the leftfield seats in hopes of catching a piece of history. Still, they joined the rest of the stadium in their wild ecstasy. After all, at least they had SEEN an Aaron home run.

Not to be forgotten as a fielder, Aaron gave his fans more to cheer about in the eighth, when he made a shoestring catch of a sinking liner off the bat of Houston's Greg Gross.

Facing righthander Larry Dierker in the last of the eighth, Aaron blooped a single to left. It was his first at-bat in search of the tying homer. When he took the field in the ninth with the Braves ahead, 7-0, the fans, sensing he would not bat again that night, gave him a rousing ovation, holding up the game several minutes as Hank waved and doffed his cap. It was a highly charged moment, one that he will remember for a long time.

"The ovation was tremendous, great," he said later. "I just hope we get 50,000 people out here tomorrow."

Some of the fans at the game obviously thought there would be a run on Sunday's tickets. A line formed at the Advance Ticket Window by 9 p.m. Saturday, less than 30 minutes after No. 713 had become history.

By 9:30, the game was over, Aaron was in the postgame news conference, and the rain, which had threatened all evening, was coming down in torrents.

Inside, Henry admitted he had guessed correctly on the pitch which had become home run No. 713. "I was guessing slow curve ball all the time," he said. "The first time up, I got a base hit on a fastball and the second time, he walked me on several slow curve balls. The third time, I was kind of hoping he would throw the slow curve again."

He said the pitch would have been a ball if he had not swung. "The pitch I hit out tonight was not a very good pitch," he noted. "It just happened I was looking for it and happened to hit it out of the ballpark. It was way down and outside."

The Hammer took special care to point out that Dierker, the Houston reliever, didn't give him anything good to hit. "Dierker was one of those pitchers who made the statement about throwing the ball right down the middle if I got to 713," said Aaron, referring to a mid-season Associated Press story in which several top NL pitchers were quoted as saying they would throw Aaron a fat pitch for the record-breaker as a quick route to the history books. "Well, there was no truth in that at all. He was probably throwing harder to me than to anybody else."

Newsmen noted that one of Hank's more vociferous supporters in the stands that night had been Herbert Aaron, his father. After the homer, he jumped up, yelling wildly. "Oh, he was enthused before I hit it," the younger Aaron said with a laugh.

It was a happy night for The Hammer and his family, but it opened the door to a game that might be his biggest challenge.

"Tomorrow is probably going to be the test I've been waiting for all these years," said Aaron. "If I get a pitch to hit, I'm going to show the world whether I'm a good hitter or not. If Dave Roberts has his breaking ball and slow curve and the other pitches he throws, and can get them over, then he can be one of the toughest left-handers in the league. He's a tremendous pitcher and the type who can send me home 0-for-4 and looking toward next year to get the home run I need to tie Babe Ruth."

Asked if he would be too nervous to sleep Saturday night, Henry responded, "I never have any trouble sleeping." The newsmen

Larry Dierker pitched cautiously to Hank despite "I'll groove it" statement.

laughed.

In marked contrast to the air of victory on the Atlanta side, Jerry Reuss reluctantly answered questions in a somber Houston clubhouse. "I wanted to get him out just as badly as he wants the record," said the pitcher. "I don't want to share the spotlight with him at all. I hate this. I realize you guys have a job to do but he's hit home runs off 700 other guys too."

SUNDAY, SEPTEMBER 30

The weatherman is probably not a baseball fan, or at least not a Braves' fan. The forecast for Sunday called for a 90 per cent chance of afternoon showers. The day began with a bright sun, blue sky, and a few puffy clouds. By game time, 2:15, the weather could best be described as threatening.

Before the game, Houston pitcher Dave Roberts, the first starting pitcher to face Hank Aaron with the record on the line, drew a line of defiance.

"I'd rather be a nobody in baseball forever than go down as an immortal because I served one of the big ones to Henry," he said. "He got his 712th off me in Houston the other night and that made me mad because it

was a 3-run job that beat us.

"I would rather not be known the way Tracy Stallard was for serving up Roger Maris' 61st in 1961. I'd rather be known for striking Aaron out and keeping him from breaking the record. I thought what Henry said on TV was interesting—that he'd probably tie or break the record off some over-powering pitcher, someone who'll challenge him. I'm not that kind of pitcher. I don't have overpowering stuff and I won't challenge him. I keep the ball down, mix speeds, and use the sinker a lot. I never threw a fat pitch in baseball intentionally and I won't now. My job is to get everybody out—and that's just what I'll try to do. After today, I hope I can look at the 1974 schedule and see who Hank gets the first shot at, because he's going to break the record off somebody. I just hope it's not Houston."

Going into Sunday's game, Roberts, with 16 wins, had a chance to set a Houston club record for wins by lefthanded pitchers. "If he comes up at any time with a chance to beat me with a home run, I'll pitch around him," said Dave, whose 1973 gopher ball to Aaron was the fifth of his career in the NL.

The game began, as scheduled, at 2:15, though

the clustering clouds made it obvious that the weather would not hold for the course of a nine-inning game, even if it were a low-scoring contest.

In the first inning, with Houston ahead, 1-0, Aaron came up with a man at third and two out. The Hammer took a big cut, but topped the ball down the third base line. He beat it out for an infield hit—to the pleasure of the crowd—and recorded his 96th run batted in of the season. It was to be his last in 1973.

Hank went 3-for-4 that afternoon, though a steady rain fell during the second half of the game. Only fireballer Don Wilson, a starter used in relief, managed to get him out—on an infield pop in the eighth. The three hits gave Aaron a .301 average for the season.

"I am disappointed, yes," Hank said afterward. "But I feel like I got all winter to go home and rest up. It's been a tiresome year for me, really. The last month, I'd say it's been really tiresome—just the same things over and over—and I'm a little relieved now that it's over. Also, I can look back now and say I had a good year."

Hank had hoped to please the 40,517 fans in the stadium with an historic homer, and admitted he took home run cuts. "I was going for home runs all the way," he said. "I wasn't thinking about the base hits, even though I knew I was close to three hundred."

Aaron conceded that a Georgia State University computer had correctly predicted he would have 713 home runs on the last day of the 1973 season. "I just refused to believe the computer," he smiled, "but evidently it was right. I went into today's game determined to hit a home run and it just didn't work that way. I wasn't nervous at all. Yesterday I was nervous because I felt like I had to hit a home run just to have the chance to tie today. But today I felt like there was no pressure at all."

According to Aaron, Roberts threw only one strike—during his first at-bat of the afternoon. "The rest were bad balls, even the ones I got hits on," he said. "He just refused to throw the ball down the middle. That first time, the umpire gave him a ball, he looked around and started laughing. I think he used reverse psychology on me because I was sure he'd throw a change-up on me but he threw it right down the middle. From then on, everything was away, away, up, away."

Dave Roberts gave up three hits to Aaron in finale—but none was a homer.

Of Don Wilson, Aaron said, "I only saw the one pitch, a bad ball, way inside. I should have taken a pitch, but usually he tries to get ahead of me with fastballs and I was anticipating a fastball somewhere on the inside part of the plate but up. He got it down and I just didn't get my bat on it. At least, I got the wrong part of the bat on it."

With the end of the season, Aaron, the modest, quiet leader of the Braves, took time to praise several of the team's younger players.

"The competition between the three of us was great," said Aaron, referring to a three-way race for the team (and league) home run crown involving Braves Darrell Evans and Dave Johnson. "I was happy to see Darrell have the kind of season he had simply because players like Darrell and Dusty Baker are the future of the Atlanta Braves."

A writer asked Aaron what he had contributed to baseball. "That's a new one," the slugger laughed. "I haven't heard that one before." He thought for a minute, then said, "I should hope that this chase of Babe Ruth's record has brought out some new fans. At the beginning of the season, a lot of people, especially the older generation, had some ideas that they didn't want me to break the record. But I got a lot of mail from the younger generation who say that this is what they want—they want to see me break the record and be able to say that they saw me play rather than think about what their grandfathers said about Babe Ruth forty years ago."

Aaron thanked the nearly 150 newsmen in the room and slipped through the side door into the Braves' locker room which was adjacent to the conference room. It would be a long winter of wondering for Aaron and the men who write and talk about him. The only question would not be if, but when. . .●

THE LONGEST SEASON

■ For Henry Aaron, the 1973 season was the longest of his 20 seasons in the major leagues.

When the Braves gathered in West Palm Beach, Fla., for the opening of their spring training camp in February, 41 home runs separated Henry Aaron from Babe Ruth. The countdown was set to begin, although there would be numerous obstacles along the way.

Aaron had hit just 34 homers and recorded his career-low average of .265 in 1972, but he still had secret hopes of tying Ruth's record and possibly breaking it in 1973. To tie, he needed 41 homers, 42 to break.

The most important fact of life for Aaron, as spring training began, was that the braves had made numerous off-season trades and apparently fortified a questionable pitching staff, as well as improving the vital up-the-middle defense. Hank knew a good showing by the pitchers could bring the National League pennant to Atlanta for the first time and enable him to play in another World Series before his career ended.

Spring training seldom attracts the national news media except for occasional writers from The Sporting News, Sports Illustrated, and the wire services, but the Braves' 1973 camp was different. Hank Aaron was getting a glimpse of things to come—of the news crush which would envelop him as the season wore on. He didn't like it and, at times, it showed. Always a quiet, private person, he seemed reluctant at times to answer questions, even from reporters he knew.

Perhaps he was reacting to hearing the same questions over and over. Why did you hit just .265? Do you think you can hit 34 home runs again? Will you get less good pitches to hit now that Earl Williams has been traded?

Yet, Hank Aaron eventually satisfied the men who came to cover him. He answered the questions in detail—except when it came to financial arrangements. His agent had advised him not to divulge money

Pressure was Hank Aaron's constant companion from the very first day in 1973.

matters to newsmen.

He talked about the disappointing 1972 season, which began with a controversial player strike that cost each club about eight dates at the start of the schedule. After the settlement, the games were not made up.

The strike began April 1, just as Aaron and other veteran players were beginning to sharpen their batting eyes for the grueling campaign ahead. The two-week layoff proved very costly.

"When the 1972 season opened," Aaron recalls, "it was like starting spring training all over again. I had lost the edge I gained in the first four weeks of training. The strike really hurt. It takes me every bit of six weeks to be in top shape when the regular season opens."

As he feared, Hank got off to a slow start in 1972—the worst slump of his career, in fact. He managed only five singles in his first 50 at-bats. Some fans started wondering if he was through, but he soon proved them wrong.

"I thought at one point I was about to start hitting for average," said the veteran star, "but I wasn't consistent and was definitely disappointed in my average. But I

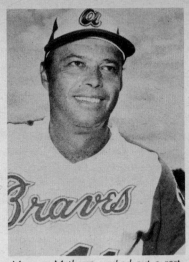

Manager Mathews worked out a rest schedule for Aaron during '73 season.

figure my main jobs have always been knocking in and scoring runs—not hitting for average.

"I didn't think there was anything wrong with my reflexes but I did have a tendency to get tired in 1972. I was over-tired a couple of times and it took me awhile to bounce back."

When former teammate Eddie Mathews took over the Atlanta mangerial job in August 1972, he worked with Henry to coordinate a program of regular rest days for the slugging star, but by that time the 1972 season was a lost one for both the team and for Aaron.

In spring training, Mathews and Aaron decided on a

definite playing schedule which usually meant days off after night games and playing in only one game of doubleheaders.

Knowing he would have time to rest and regain his strength on the bench in 1973 was a psychological boost to Aaron, who played too often in 1972 in a last-ditch effort to save Luman Harris' job as manager. One man—even Aaron—couldn't accomplish the mission alone, though, and Harris was gone shortly after the All-Star Game in Atlanta.

The firing of Harris and hiring of Mathews represented the first salvoes in a wholesale shakeup of the Braves which began immediately after the 1972 season. Three solid hitters—Earl Williams, Rico Carty, and Felix Millan—were the key figures in trades which brought a half-dozen pitchers, a first-string second baseman, and a fine defensive catcher to Atlanta. But the deals seemed to leave such a void in the Atlanta offense that pitchers could work around Aaron without giving him anything good to hit.

Reporters asked his opinion. "The trades don't bother me," he responded. "I've been playing too long to let something like that affect

me. I have to discipline myself so that whoever is hitting behind me—whether it's Earl Williams or Dusty Baker, or whoever it is—I'm gonna go up there and do my thing regardless of what they do.

"We got four good ballplayers and certainly improved our team," he continued, discussing the trade of Williams and hot minor-league prospect Taylor Duncan to Baltimore for pitchers Pat Dobson and Roric Harrison, catcher Johnny Oates, and second baseman Dave Johnson.

"Anytime you get four starters for one regular, you feel like you've helped yourself tremendously."

Then Aaron underlined his feelings with a prediction. "This is a fine ballclub and we have a chance of winning our division," he said. "Everybody in camp feels like we can win."

On paper, it appeared Hank was right. But it was not to be a championship year for Atlanta—or even a .500 year.

Dobson got off to a 3-7 start and was dealt to the Yankees for Frank Tepedino, a young lefthanded power-hitter who plays first base, and three minor leaguers. Harrison began in the bullpen, pitched brilliantly, and earned a spot in the starting rotation. Then he ran into injuries. He had a dismal second half of the season.

Gary Gentry and Danny Frisella, two hard-throwing righthanders obtained from the New York Mets, won a combined total of five games and lost eight before both went on the disabled list with arm troubles that necessitated operations.

Pitching ace Phil Niekro missed most of spring training with arm problems, then reached the climax of a good season with the National League's only no-hitter in early August. Then, mysteriously, he won just two games the rest of the season.

The Braves' defense was spotty, especially after Oates was shelved for the season with a mid-July injury. He had just begun to learn the idiosyncracies of the Atlanta pitchers and had developed good rapport with them.

Without Frisella, expected to be the top relief pitcher, the team had no bullpen to speak of and was forced to carry a number of inexperienced hurlers getting on-the-job training under the pressure of major-league bats.

With all these problems, the Braves finished fifth in the six-team National League West. Yet, they lead the league in homers, runs scored, runs batted in, and team batting. In pitching and defense, Atlanta ranked last in the 12-team circuit.

Since the Braves' problems started early in the year, and the team dropped far off the pennant chase before school was out, the sole attention of the media was concentrated on Hank Aaron. The great outfielder might have had the undivided attention of the press anyhow, but since he was the only big story on the Braves—excepting the surprising home run pace of Dave Johnson—he commanded the headlines . . . day in and day out.

For Aaron, the 1973 season began with the spring announcement by Eddie Mathews that Hank was being moved back to the outfield after two years at first base. The move was welcomed by Henry, who reported, "I'm through making a fool of myself as a first baseman. Anybody who thinks he's making it easy by putting an older player at first is crazy.

"When I'm in the outfield, I can relax between pitches. It gives me time to reflect between strikeouts, wondering what's going wrong. I'm sure that when the Braves put me in the lineup as a first baseman, they figured it would save my legs. Maybe that's true, but that's all it saves. It almost ran my head crazy."

Mathews explained the move: "We felt it would help our ballclub and help Henry at the same time. That's where he's played all his life (the outfield) and it's an easier position than first base. He's very agreeable to it."

Though The Hammer opened in rightfield with speedy Ralph Garr in left, the two men switched spots May 4 in Philadelphia because Garr, with the more powerful throwing arm, could make the rifle throws from right to third base, while Aaron couldn't. A leftfielder is not required to make the long-distance throws that a rightfielder must execute.

The move had been contemplated by Mathews for some time during the season's first month, but wasn't finalized until Montreal base-runners took some liberties with Aaron's arm at the suggestion of Expos pilot Gene Mauch. Though Mauch insisted he still had the highest respect for Hank's bat, he underlined the obvious by showing Aaron, at 39, couldn't cut it anymore as a rightfielder.

Though he got off to a good

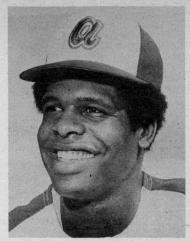

The trade of Earl Williams after 1972 left a void in the Atlanta attack.

start in home run production, Aaron was not hitting for average. On June 21, he had an anemic .219 mark, hardly fitting for a man whose 19-year career percentage was .311, best in the league. Aaron, realizing he was in an embarrassing situation, decided to do something about it. He began to swing the bat.

On July 8, he picked on ex-teammate George Stone, a lefthander pitching for the New York Mets, for a pair of home runs as the Braves ran up a 4-2 victory at Shea Stadium. The first disappeared in the leftfield seats, just a few feet from the foul pole, while the second struck a seat in the mezzanine deck and bounced back onto the field. The 33,000 fans at the park gave Hank a standing ovation and he said later, "I wasn't surprised. New York is one of my favorite places to play."

The Hammer said Stone threw him two bad pitches for his home runs. "Neither pitch was down the middle," said the slugger, who'd been saying all season that he no longer sees anything in the strike zone. "The first homer, in the fourth, was on a change-up curve that was a good low pitch. The second, in the sixth, was off a fastball. Neither pitch was in the strike zone. I don't see pitches down the middle anymore—not even in batting practice."

A writer tried to get Aaron to brand himself a bad-ball hitter, a title currently reserved for Pittsburgh's Manny Sanguillen. Aaron didn't grab the bait however. "I've had my pitches, too," he said.

His two-homer game against the Mets July 8 was Aaron's third of the season and increased his seasonal total to 23 and career output to 696. Earlier, Hank had homered twice in the same game on May 1, connecting against Balor Moore and John Strohmayer of Mon-

treal, and again on June 9, against Scipio Spinks and John Andrews of St. Louis. On May 13, he homered in each game of a doubleheader against San Diego, as a pinch-hitter against Bill Greif in the ninth inning of the opener and in a starting role against Fred Norman in the nightcap. On Sept. 3, Aaron also hit two homers in one game, picking on the Padres' Clay Kirby and Vicente Romo.

In three of the four instances when Hank slammed two home runs in the same game, he accomplished the feat at Atlanta Stadium, the park where he delivered 26 of his 40 homers during the 1973 season.

Because the Braves were doing poorly, and because Atlanta has proven itself a better town for football than for baseball, Aaron's heroics at home were seen by relatively few fans. The Braves drew only 800,678 for the season, just slightly better than their 1972 draw and the 11th worst in the league. Only San Diego, where rumors of a franchise shift ran rampant all year, played before fewer fans at home: 611,827.

"Oh, sure you're disappointed at small crowds," Aaron confessed, "but being

Aaron rounds third, touches home and holds ball aloft after hitting No. 700.

a professional you have to go out and play whether you have 1,300 or 52,000. I feel 1,300 are entitled to see you play—if that's all there are—just as hard as you always play."

Just 16,236 fans witnessed one of the highlights of Aaron's year—his 700th home run July 21, a 400-foot shot off lefthander Ken Brett of Philadelphia (now Pittsburgh) at Atlanta Stadium. The blow came with a man on base in the third inning of a game the Braves eventually lost, 8-4.

Though he and Babe Ruth are the only players ever to hit the 700 mark, Aaron poo-pooed the event. "I don't feel any special thrill," he said afterward. "It's just a number. The big one is THE one."

But Darrell Evans, on base at the time, said Aaron was shaking when he crossed the plate. "It was the first time I've seen him become really emotional," said Evans, who blossomed into a home run star in his own right in 1973.

Aaron, surrounded by reporters in the clubhouse after the game, said he knew the ball would go out of the park. "I knew it was gone," he said. "When you hit 700, you know when you hit one that will go."

The blow, his 27th of the season, gave him two full months to aim for the magic 714. "I wanted to hit number seven hundred before the All-Star break," said the slugger, whose bags were already packed for the trip to Kansas City the following evening. "That sounds a little better—only fourteen to go. Not like sixteen or eighteen. I think maybe I can do it now. I thought when the season started I could hit about 35 home runs. Nothing surprises me. When you've been playing the game as long as I have, you're not surprised by too much."

Phil Niekro, the veteran Atlanta pitcher, spent the game on the dugout bench, watching Aaron and waiting. "Everybody in the dugout was waiting silently when he went to bat," he said. "You knew it was going to happen. It was just a matter of time."

Meanwhile, Philadelphia's winning pitcher, Ken Brett, said, "The score was 8-4, our favor, and I wouldn't have cared if he hit four. If I can go into the record book every time winning, the homers won't bother me at all."

The young southpaw said he was well aware of the home run's significance because a capricious teammate had taped the number "700" on his locker before the game.

Billye Williams, then Hank's fiancee, missed his historic 700th home run.

seats in the leftfield bleachers, Aaron's favorite home run spot.

One important fan who missed even a glimpse of the home run was Billye Williams, Atlanta television hostess who was then Aaron's fiancee and is now his second wife.

"I thought the game was supposed to start at seven," she said, "but actually it started an hour earlier. As a result, I wasn't in the ballpark when Henry hit that homer in the third inning."

Whether they were there or not, fans from all over the country wrote or wired Aaron their congratulations. Jack Benny, who until last season was the world's most famous 39-year-old, was one individual turned on by Aaron. "The title is his now," said Benny, whose violin is as destructive an instrument as Aaron's bat. "He deserves it. I'm pulling for him to break the record."

Frank Sinatra was among a host of well-known persons to send a wire. President Nixon did not, but Hank was willing to excuse him. "He has enough problems," explained the tactful athlete.

One person Henry didn't excuse was Baseball Commissioner Bowie Kuhn who, like the President, did not send a congratulatory

"I wasn't going to pitch around him because the guy hitting behind him—Dusty Baker—is one of the best hitters in baseball. But I'll say this—it was the first homer he's hit off me and it'll be the last."

The fan who claimed the ball, 18-year-old Robert Winborne of Atlanta, was given 700 silver dollars by the Braves' management in exchange for the ball. The University of North Carolina freshman said he didn't let other fans know he had caught the historic ball. "I just sat there, hugging it," he revealed. "I didn't even tell my friends." He made the catch inside a pile of fans who deliberately bought telegram. "I thought I would have received a telegram from the Commissioner," Aaron said, pointing out that National League president Chub Feeney had sent one. "I felt let down. Regardless of how small he thought it was, it wasn't small to me. I think what I did was good for baseball."

Aaron made such a fuss over the Commissioner's failure to wire that the baseball czar, put on the defensive, issued a special statement at the All-Star Game, three days after the milestone home run, saying no slight had been intended.

"I'm certainly sorry that Hank Aaron was disappointed as I am sure he knows I am one of his biggest rooters," said Kuhn. "I want to lead the baseball world in celebration when he hits 714 and 715."

The Commissioner even made a special trip to see Aaron in St. Louis when the Braves were there shortly after the slugger had reached the 700 milestone.

"I explained to him I very rarely give out congratulations on particular achievements because there are so many of them that you're always going to run the risk of offending someone you didn't remember," Kuhn recalled. "Furthermore, I told him I planned to break the rule when Henry hit 714 and 715 as I knew he would."

Aaron stood his ground. "I understood his position and he understood mine," the star said after his meeting with baseball's chief executive. "My statement was that it would be a long time before he saw anyone hit 700 home runs again and I didn't think one telegram would hurt."

Several writers leaped to Kuhn's defense in the controversy. They explained that it was not the Commissioner's place to congratulate a National Leaguer for achieving a mark only an American Leaguer had reached before, whereas NL president Feeney should boost players from his own league.

These journalists wrote that the Commissioner should be as neutral in the Aaron-Ruth controversy as he is in the World Series or All-Star Game. It was a logical explanation, but so was Aaron's claim that what he did was good for modern-day baseball.

The telegram episode soon passed and Henry Aaron moved on to other things.

The bat used to hammer No. 700 went to Louisville rather than the Baseball Hall of Fame. "That was part of a contract I have with the bat company," said Aaron. "I've sent several things to the Hall of Fame, but they're not listed. The ball and bat from my 3,000th hit, the balls for my 500th and 600th home runs—none of them were in the brochure the last time I looked. I've decided to hold onto the 700th home run ball for the time being."

The slugger was so irritated by the oversight from Cooperstown that he even threatened to withhold future mementoes, possibly including the bats and balls involved in the tying and breaking of Babe Ruth's record. Ken Smith, the Hall's Director, promised to correct the omissions involving Aaron's achievements and donations.

Aaron got a welcome break after hitting his 700th homer—he got three days off from the grind of the 162-game National League schedule. He was voted to the NL's All-Star lineup, and insisted he welcomed the opportunity to play in the game. It was his 19th straight All-Star assignment.

"If I were home looking at the game on TV, I'd be wishing I were here," he said after arriving in Kansas City for the July 24 classic. "I'd rather be here than fishing. There will be plenty of time for that later on."

Henry made a prophetic statement to reporters covering the game. He said his record-breaking home run would probably come in 1974. "It figures to be the first part of next year before I hit it," he said, modifying a statement he had made after his 700th homer just three days earlier.

This time, Aaron and the Georgia State computer agreed. The computer which belched forth predictions about the Aaron/Ruth race, was the one thing which seemed to bug Aaron more than the tape recorders and microphones. It operated on a matrix of information fed to it by Dr. Lester Sartorius and other professors, and based its forecasts on the last 13 years of Hank's career, 1961-1973.

After Hank hit No. 701 off Cincinnati's Pedro Borbon on July 31, 10 days after hitting No. 700 off Philadelphia's Ken Brett, the computer laid 3-to-1 odds that the record would not be broken in 1973. It was on Aug. 1 that the computer made a startling prediction—it said that going into the last game of the season, Hank Aaron would have 713 home runs. That's exactly how it turned out, although the probability changed every time Aaron connected.

"Every time he hits a homer or makes an out, the probability changes," explained Dr. Sartorius. "One factor we can't measure is whether the pitchers are making it harder for him to connect. Another is the emotional factor."

Both Aaron and Eddie Mathews said the pitchers tended to work harder on The Hammer after he passed the 700 milestone.

"Reaching seven hundred wasn't really all that tough," said the slugger, looking back on his long career. "But now the pitchers are concentrating a little more when I get up to the plate. It's going to be harder than a lot of people think for me to break the record this season."

Mathews explained, "I've noticed the pitchers are trying harder when Henry comes up. They're not pitching around him, but they seem to be putting a little extra on the ball. No one wants to be the guy who throws the ball as he gets closer."

The manager knew what he was talking about; there was a drought of 17 days— Hank's longest dry spell of the season—between home runs 701 and 702. He did hit one homer during the span, but it came in an exhibition

"Henry Aaron knows I'm one of his biggest rooters," said Bowie Kuhn.

game played before Aaron's old fans in Milwaukee. The Braves-Brewers game has been an annual affair at Milwaukee County Stadium and took on added significance in 1973, the year Aaron narrowed the gap between himself and Babe Ruth.

"You know, there were over 33,000 people there and half of them came out there to see me," said Aaron after the game, won by the Brewers, who began life as the Seattle Pilots, a 1969 American League expansion team. "I came back after eight years and they were standing up over two minutes for me. That brought tears to my eyes."

Aaron, who connected with a Bill Parsons fast ball in the sixth inning, said after the game that he would like to return to Milwaukee in a front-office capacity after his playing career ends.

"I've got to eat," he told the Milwaukee press corps. "I've got to support my family and have a job. And I promise to work as hard being in the front office as I did when I was a player. If I had a choice, it would be Milwaukee."

That date—Aug. 6, 1973—was a big one for Aaron's fans in the Upper Midwest. Wisconsin Gov. Patrick Lucey declared it Hank Aaron Day and the fans turned out to honor the former kingpin of the Milwaukee Braves. Many of the old heroes were there—in addition to Aaron, Braves' manager Eddie Mathews and pitching coach Lew Burdette and Brewers' manager Del Crandall who were all instrumental in the 1957 and 1958 pennants that flew over Milwaukee County Stadium.

Ten days after the fete in Milwaukee, Hank Aaron ended his regular-season home run dry spell by belting a 400-foot drive off Cubs' reliever Jack Aker with two teammates on base. The clout cleared the leftfield bleachers at Wrigley Field and highlighted a nine-run

eighth inning as Atlanta won, 10-2.

"I've been concentrating on getting my timing back," said Aaron after the game. "I haven't been swinging good."

The blow was the first in a flurry of home runs for Hank, who tends to hit them in clusters, a trait of a guess hitter in the groove. No. 703 came the next day, at Montreal, and No. 704 the day after.

Aaron's 704th was also his 1,387th extra-base hit, moving the Atlanta star into first place—ahead of Stan Musial—on the all-time list in that department.

"This was very important for me," said Aaron, who jumped on the first pitch by Montreal rookie Steve Rogers in the eighth inning. "It is a tremendous achievement. You know, getting that many extra-base hits means even more to me than 714 or 715 home runs. This is the only ball I've ever wanted to keep."

The Hammer delivered six more home runs in late August and early September and, by Sept. 10, when the Braves opened a three-game series with San Francisco in Atlanta, he needed just five home runs to tie Babe Ruth.

By the time that game was over, the countdown had reached four, but Hank

Aaron was under medication. The team said the problem was stomach cramps.

"Hank had severe stomach cramps, so they took him to a doctor," said Mathews, who had witnessed home run No. 710 before the stomach ailment knocked Aaron out of the lineup. "The doctor called about 11 o'clock and said he was okay."

Teammate Dave Johnson said, "He's been having a little problem lately with his stomach. I think he has cramps in his side. I don't think it's nervousness, but I sure wouldn't blame him if it were."

The Associated Press expounded on Aaron's amazing resiliency in its recount of the game. The AP story began, "Neither wind, nor rain, nor Don Carrithers could stay Hank Aaron from No. 710 . . . but stomach cramps kept the Atlanta slugger from his next appointed round-tripper."

By Sept. 14, Hank was fully recuperated and was in the lineup as the Braves opened a weekend series at Cincinnati's Riverfront Stadium. Four home runs would tie Babe Ruth.

The leftfield seats were gone well before the opening game of the series. "I've never seen anything like it," said Dale Stoeber, Cin-

cinnati's director of ticket services. "We've been selling leftfield tickets for the past month and a half, and we've had requests from as far away as Iowa and New York."

Another Red official said, "They're crazy. Somebody's going to get killed."

Cincinnati business firms offered $1,000, $2,000, and $3,000 for Aaron home run balls. Nets were smuggled into the stand. Women wore gloves to the ballpark in the hope of catching a piece of history.

As it turned out, Henry did not connect in the Rhineland, but he didn't have to wait long for No. 711. It came Sept. 17 against San Diego's Gary Ross. No. 712 won the Sept. 22 game against Houston's Dave Roberts, who yielded it in the Astrodome with two Braves on base. Finally, Aaron closed out his long ball hitting for the season with No. 713 against Houston's Jerry Reuss Sept. 29, with two men on base in Atlanta Stadium.

Offensively, Henry Aaron's season was spectacular. His .643 slugging percentage—total bases divided by times at bat—was his second best ever (.669 in 1971 ranked higher) and his 12 game-winning hits led the Braves, though he batted just 392 times, fewest of his 20-year

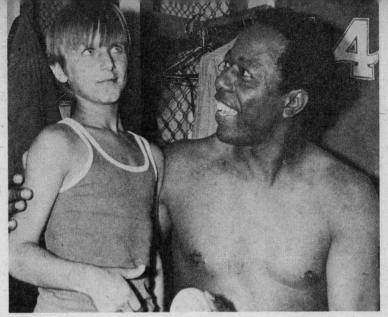

Luc Gervais, 12, meets Aaron after catching Hank's 703rd HR in Montreal.

career in the majors.

Perhaps the most amazing thing about The Hammer's all-around showing was his robust late-season hitting. From June 21 on, he hit .369. From July 24, the date of the All-Star Game, to the end of the season, he tore up NL pitching at a .398 clip. His final average of .301 marked his 14th appearance in the .300 club—a record unmatched by any major-leaguer since 1950 except Stan Musial and Ted Williams.

Aaron himself attributed his dramatic reversal at bat to his increased strength (he rested more in 1973 than in any other season) and to his intense drive for the record.

Veteran hitting instructor Dixie Walker, one-time Braves' batting coach who filled the same capacity for the Dodgers last season, was astounded by Hank's performance in 1973.

"Aaron surprised me," he said. "People asked me if I thought he could do it and I said he wouldn't come close; he'd break the record in a year or two. I played at 39 and there ain't no way he could be that strong at his age."

Another authority on hitting, Cincinnati catcher Johnny Bench, has an excellent vantage point from which to observe Aaron. Bench thinks Aaron's secret is his low-key approach. "He is one of the coolest, calmest guys I've ever known," says Johnny. "When he walks to the plate, it's just unbelievable. He does his thing in quiet. The thought of him being pressured by anything, even as he nears the record, is just, well, I can't imagine it."

Though Aaron has been accused of catching up on his sleep between pitches, he is wide awake when he uncoils that powerful swing. "I force myself to relax up there," he says, revealing one of the game's worst-kept secrets. "Maybe I don't look nervous, but I am sometimes. And I can't hit when I'm tight, so I've got to relax and loosen up. I take good care of myself. I'll go as far as my body takes me in this game. So far, it's taken good care of me, so I take good care of it.

"Yes, I think about the age thing, but there is nothing I can do about it. One day, no matter how great you are, or how great you were, you have to retire. It will be a hard decision for me, but I realize that one day it will have to happen."

All indications are that day will come soon after the end of the 1974 season. Until he hangs up his spikes, however, Hank Aaron will keep swinging.

Aaron has an unorthodox

"Aaron doesn't need help from the pitcher," maintains Mets' Tom Seaver.

swing which should not be copied by youngsters, according to some expert hitting coaches. "My right hand turns over toward the pitcher, so when I hit the ball there's a rotation on it," says Henry, who hits off his right foot, overstrides, and drags his back foot so often that his right shoe wears out before the left one.

Houston manager Preston Gomez, who replaced Leo Durocher at the end of the 1973 season, doesn't care about the unorthodox swing. He still hates to see Aaron come to the plate, and he understands why Sandy Koufax and Don Drysdale named him "Bad Henry" back in the days when Gomez was the Dodger pitching coach.

"We used to go over the opposing lineup and nobody ever wanted to pitch to Aaron," he says. "Soon all the guys were calling him 'Bad Henry' and the name spread around the league."

The Dodger pitchers, through their nickname, paid tribute to Aaron's batting excellence through the years. "Consistency is what counts," says the slugger. "You have to be able to do things over and over again."

Aaron's perennial excellence reveals one of his inner secrets: his love of the game. "When I first came into baseball," he explains, "I had a taste for it in my mouth that has never changed. I still love to play, though it gets harder with the length of the schedule, the traveling, and the night games."

Super-consistency enabled Aaron to mount his challenge to Ruth, which in 1973 reached a climax that produced two major controversies.

One concerned a torrent of anti-Aaron letters, many of them outright hate letters, received by the slugging star. "What do they want me to do?" asked Hank quizzically. "Stop hitting home runs?"

Atlanta public relations director Bob Hope noted that not all the racist letters came from the South. "We got quite a few from New York City, too," he said.

Aaron, hurt by the racial slurs directed against him, even challenged a white fan who vocalized his prejudice one night at Atlanta Stadium. Oddly, blacks living in Atlanta tend to stay away from the stadium—despite Aaron's quest for immortality. Perhaps they remember the old days of segregation at the ballpark or perhaps ticket prices are too high. The whites who see the Braves play are generally a loyal, high-spirited group, but apparently there are some rednecks in the crowd. As Aaron approached Ruth's record near the end of the '73 season, the rednecks either stayed away or kept quiet for fear of bodily harm from Hank's fans.

Early in the season, the situation involving hate mail and incidents in Atlanta became tense until the publicity generated a public outpouring of well-wishes not only from every National League city, but from all over the country. The overwhelming support for Aaron silenced most of the hate-mongers.

Hank had won the public to

his side and for a time it appeared he had won some of the pitchers too. But he didn't like that idea at all and was appalled when The Associated Press reported in mid-June that several top NL pitchers would throw Aaron a fat pitch with the tying or record-breaking home run on the line. The Atlanta star started with nothing and built himself into Babe Ruth's first serious challenger without assistance from anyone. Henry Aaron, in a nutshell, is a self-made man, and wants to keep it that way.

Aaron occasionally made reference to the story in comments to newsmen as the season progressed. Even after the next-to-last game of the season, he told of his last time at bat against Houston's Larry Dierker.

"Dierker was one of the pitchers who made the statement about throwing the ball down the middle if I get to 713," said Hank, who had hit that home run two innings before facing reliever Dierker in the eighth. "Well, anyone could see he was throwing harder to me than to anyone else, so there's no truth in that at all."

At other points during the year, Aaron also made reference to the story. "You can tell the Commissioner he

didn't lay it in there for me," he said, noting that Baseball Commissioner Bowie Kuhn had admonished the pitchers in the AP story for their alleged indiscretions.

Those quoted in the story included Reggie Cleveland, Juan Marichal, Tug McGraw, Andy Messersmith and Pete Richert. Apparently recalling that throwing a big home run pitch made household names of Tracy Stallard (Roger Maris' 61st) and Tom Zachary (Babe Ruth's 60th), Richert said, "The man who throws it will never be forgotten. I've thrown enough homers in my career, so what's another? No, I wouldn't mind throwing it."

McGraw, the Mets' colorful relief star, told the AP: "I'd throw my best pitch and hope like hell he hits it. It'd be a commodity. I'd always be in demand on the banquet circuit."

On the other hand, the vast majority of NL pitchers swore they'd do their best whenever they faced Aaron. Tom Seaver of the Mets, generally regarded as the league's premier pitcher, summed up the general feeling when he said, "If Henry Aaron gets the record off me, he would have to get it with me pitching to the absolute best of my ability. I think if any pitcher does 'give' a home run to him, he's doing a disservice to Henry Aaron. He's the type of hitter who doesn't need any help."

In addition to contending with hate mail and pitchers seeking a quick route to fame, Aaron had to learn to live with the ghost of Babe Ruth.

Aaron did not hear from Mrs. Babe Ruth during the season. "I think she has the idea I'm trying to take away some of the glory her husband had, but that's not true," he said. "You can be sure the fans are not going to forget Babe Ruth. At the same time, I don't want them to forget me."

Mrs. Ruth, hearing of Aaron's remark, responded, "This is Hank Aaron's show and I don't want to detract from it. Nobody is interested in what I have to say now."

Roger Maris, the introverted ex-slugger, who smashed a record 61 home runs in the 1961 season, visited Atlanta Stadium during the 1973 season to see Aaron play. Perhaps Maris wanted to see how Hank was reacting to the pressure applied by the media, the fans, and the aura of sports' greatest record.

"Hank will learn that the only time he's going to get any relief is when he's out on the field," said Maris, a lefthanded slugger who did not hit as many as 40 home runs in any other season during his 12-year career with the Indians, A's, Yankees and Cardinals. "Hank never will be able to enjoy himself either before or after ball games," Maris added. "He'll never be able to relax—that's how the demands for his time will be."

Aaron did run into problems in trying to protect his privacy. A group of enterprising reporters found him fishing on an off-day and a group of autograph hounds forced him to leave a Cincinnati restaurant before he could finish a cup of coffee. And, at the stadium, journalists by the dozens watched his every move.

"I can't say anything about the recognition Hank gets," said Darrell Evans, an admiring teammate who is the most logical candidate to succeed The Hammer as Atlanta's top home run star.

"Hank deserves all he gets. Besides, I kind of enjoy reading about him, too."

The writers and broadcasters are back on Aaron's trail as he nears his final objective in 1974—and so is the legendary ghost. From all appearances, 1974 will be Aaron's last, but it can hardly rival 1973 as his longest. •

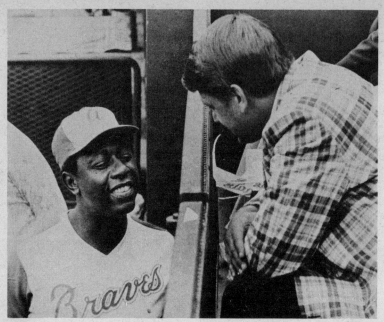

Two guys who know what pressure is all about: Aaron (L) and Roger Maris.

FIGHTING THE PRESSURE

■ The pressure of Hank Aaron's challenge to Babe Ruth can best be compared with the weather. It's easy to complain about it but impossible to do anything about it.

The pressure wrapped itself around Aaron like a thick fog even before the first ball was thrown at the Braves' spring training camp. The press, the fans, and the men who play baseball all knew that in 1973, for the first time, it was possible for someone to pass Babe Ruth in lifetime home runs.

According to Eddie Mathews, no one in the game was better prepared for the pressures of the final drive toward Ruth's record.

"Hank has known pressure all his life," said the manager. "He went through hell just like Jackie Robinson did. There were still plenty of 'white only' hotels and restaurants when Hank broke in with the Braves in 1954 but he managed to take it and keep his head above water.

"He isn't outspoken but he has fought in his own way to better conditions for black Americans and he has seen many important changes. That's one reason why he doesn't understand some of the things that upset the new generation of players. Hank has been through so much that he doesn't understand why some of the current fellows complain about the type of soap in the shower room or the location of their lockers."

Mathews, who was the only man to play for the Braves in Boston, Milwaukee and Atlanta, said spring training conditions in the mid-1950s were bad for blacks.

"One time in Bradenton, Fla., Hank, Bob Buhl and I were walking along the street and I suggested we have a beer," Mathews related. Aaron didn't like the idea, and Mathews and Buhl, both muscular athletes, immediately realized why. "He thought he would be refused service because he is black," Mathews continued. "We told him we wouldn't go in if he didn't go in with us."

The three men did go in and the bartender, perhaps after surveying the three powerful ballplayers, served them all.

Such an incident can severaly damage a young, impressionable player and Aaron, who came up at age 20, was one of the youngest in the NL in the mid-1950s. Yet, then as now, he handled the pressure well.

"The simple fact," said Mathews, "is that Hank already has handled much greater pressures than those which he is experiencing as he nears Ruth's mark."

Today, Aaron feels the primary pressure comes from the stands. "They expect me to hit a home run every time up," he says. "Of course, you try your best every time, but it's impossible to hit a home run all the time. Sometimes you get a big base hit and they're disappointed."

The Hammer's reaction to those who don't want him to break Ruth's record is understandable. He just tries to forget about them.

"I don't care what the people say, I really don't," he maintains. "Baseball has changed in such a way that regardless of whether I hit eight hundred home runs or seven-fifty, I just have to go out and have myself a good career and forget about what the fans think."

Though Hank insists the platoon of reporters assigned to him doesn't impose any great pressure, he admits he got a break by signing with the Braves instead of a New York club.

"If I were with the Yankees or Mets, I'd probably have the same fifteen or twenty writers asking me the same questions all the time," he said early in the 1973 season, before the nation's press began saturating the sports pages with Aaron stories. "I'm sure I'm not going to feel the pressure as much as if I were playing in a large city."

Referring to Roger Maris' assault on Ruth's single-season mark of 60 homers (Maris finally hit 61 in 1961) Aaron observed, "If Roger Maris were playing in any other city than New York, he would have taken the pressure as well as anyone. If I was playing in New York, I probably couldn't take it either. But I have a break there."

Maris remembers. "The pressure was terrific. Mentally much more than physically. You have no idea what it was like to put up with something like that for two months. People around you all the time. You can't

New York-based publicity for heroes like Willie Mays often irked Aaron.

eat, you can't sleep, you can't even think! I wish I had done it in my last year," continues the former Yankee outfielder, who says the Aaron race has created pressure for him again because his office phone never stops ringing with questions from reporters. "I can't say I enjoyed those last seven years of my career in baseball. If something like that happens, it would be nice to have it come that last year, then get out of the game. You just don't get any peace of mind."

Maris' 60th came off Baltimore righthander Jack Fisher, who later reached baseball notoriety as a big loser for the New York Mets.

Not playing in New York enabled Aaron to thrive in cities like Milwaukee and Atlanta, where he compiled an outstanding record each season, but avoided the national press spotlight reserved for New York heroes like Willie Mays and Mickey Mantle. Aaron knew he had been overlooked for many years, despite posting credentials superior to Mays and Mantle in quite a number of seasons.

"I've always read Mickey Mantle, Willie Mays and then Hank Aaron," he says. "I've worked awfully hard to get my name up front."

Now that he has succeeded, he is the focal point of the greatest story in baseball history primarily because he is challenging baseball's greatest hero at a time when America badly needs new heroes.

For years, writers had thought Mays would be Ruth's successor but time caught up with Willie and Aaron passed him in career home runs on June 10, 1972, when he belted No. 649 off Philadelphia's Wayne Twitchell.

"You guys were thinking about Willie Mays," Hank told reporters asking about the race with Ruth. "I was thinking about myself." By the beginning of the 1973 season, so was everybody else. "I have much less time to myself now," he admitted. "I think I could have attended a banquet every night last winter and people are always asking me to make public appearances. I just don't have enough time to satisfy everyone. I need some time to myself—like anyone else—to relax physically and mentally."

Yet, Aaron got little respite from his race with destiny as the 1973 campaign progressed. "Not a day goes by that I don't hear the name Babe Ruth," he said one night before a game at Atlanta Stadium.

Babe's widow, Mrs. Clara Ruth, even felt the heat of the sudden intense publicity. "I just want some peace of mind," she said in late summer 1973. "I'm fed up with it. I don't think it's good taste for me to intrude. It takes something away from the dignity of what Mr. Aaron is trying to do. I have made seven trips on behalf of the Babe Ruth League and everywhere I go, there are the same old questions and answers. I am besieged for interviews and public appearances."

One of Mrs. Babe Ruth's happier appearances during the 1973 season occurred when Yankee Stadium held a "Babe Ruth Day," giving fans at that day's game special Babe Ruth pictures and records. Perhaps, for Mrs. Ruth at least, it brought back some of the past glory and shifted the spotlight temporarily away from her husband's challenger.

The women around the home run kings always feel the pressure. Aaron's fiancee, Mrs. Billye Williams, felt the vise of constant public exposure closing in around her in 1973. "It's like living in a fishbowl," she confided. "I'm pleased he's finally getting the recognition he deserves but people are fickle. Today's fans may be gone tomorrow. Since Henry's not the flamboyant type, I don't think breaking the record will generate as much attention as it might have."

The popular hostess of the "Today in Georgia" television show is the widow of Dr. Samuel Williams, co-founder of the Southern Christian Leadership Conference and a well-known Atlanta civil rights leader who once taught Dr. Martin Luther King Jr.

"Samuel was very much in the public eye," she recalls. "He was always being quoted in the papers and I was involved in fund-raising work with him. But it never got into my private life."

Cecile Williams, Billye's 8-year-old daughter, and Aaron's four children by his first marriage have all adjusted well to being in the spotlight. So has Hank, according to Billye. "Cecile is an avid fan of Henry's, as are all his children," she says. "And he is unbelievably calm. He handles the pressure well—far better than I do."

For the 40-year-old outfielder, pressure is hardly new. In addition to the problems of segregation early in his career, Aaron has faced and overcome many stiff challenges in his 20-year march through National League pitching.

In his rookie year of 1954, Hank seized a golden opportunity to win a regular job when Bobby Thomson, who had just been acquired to play the outfield for the Braves, broke an ankle in spring training. Aaron, primarily an infielder, switched to the outfield and collected three hits in his first spring training start after the Thomson accident.

In 1956, at the age of 22, he won his first batting title with a .328 average as the Braves narrowly missed bringing the first NL pennant to Milwaukee. In 1957, Aaron, not one to let the same pitch or the same opportunity slip by twice, matched his uniform number with 44 home runs, collected his career-high 132 runs batted in, and batted .322 to lead the Braves to the flag. He personally assured the championship when he swatted a two-run homer in the 11th inning against Billy Muffett of St. Louis to give the Braves a flag-clinching 4-2 victory Sept. 23.

The pressure increased for the 23-year-old Milwaukee outfielder in the World Series against the New York Yankees. And, as always, he responded well, hitting a robust .393 with three home runs in the seven-game classic, which went to the Braves.

Another banner year brought Milwaukee another flag in 1958 and Aaron's .333 World Series average showed, once again, that he could handle World Series pressure.

Then, in 1959, Hank enjoyed what he calls his greatest year for hitting the ball. He began like an ICBM headed for a distant target. His average stayed well over .400 until mid-June, when he sprained his ankle in Philadelphia's Connie Mack Stadium while chasing a fly ball. He finished with a blistering .355 mark, slugged 39 home runs, and knocked in 123 runs. The Braves tied for first with the Dodgers, then lost the post-season playoff for the pennant.

It was during the 1959 season that Aaron enjoyed his greatest single day at the plate. It came in San Francisco's Seals Stadium, an old minor league park being used by the Giants pending the completion of Candlestick Park in 1960. Seals Stadium was one of Aaron's favorite places to play because it was ideally suited to righthanded power-hitters. In the first, the powerful Milwaukee slugger connected off lefthander Johnny Antonelli with one man on. He hit another homer off Stu Miller, a righty, with one on in the sixth, and a third in the seventh against another reliever, Gordon Jones, also with one man on base.

A month before his three-home run outburst on June 21, Hank became a part of baseball history through a rare base-running error. On the evening of May 26, Harvey Haddix, Pittsburgh lefthander, had hurled 12 perfect innings against the Braves in Milwaukee, but had not won because Braves' righthander Lew Burdette, the gutsy veteran, had scattered 12 hits without

Vida Blue was victim of Hank Aaron's first All-Star Game homer in 1971.

permitting a run.

In the last of the 13th, Felix Mantilla led off and was safe on an error by Don Hoak, ending the perfect game but not the no-hitter. Eddie Mathews sacrificed Mantilla to second. Aaron was up with one out. Haddix, with the perfect game gone anyhow, walked him intentionally to set up the possibility of an inning-ending double-play. With lumbering Joe Adcock at the plate, the odds were good that any ground ball would do the trick for the Pirates.

But Adcock crossed up the strategy. He hit the ball out of the park for what appeared to be a game-ending three-run homer. That's when the excited Aaron, as startled as anyone in the park at the shock ending of the game, cut across the diamond and ran into the dugout after touching second. He never completed the curcuit around the bases. But Adcock, who had homered, did and was technically out for passing Aaron on the basepaths.

The Braves had won—everyone knew that—but the score was in doubt until a final ruling came down a day later. Adcock would be credited with a double, driving home Mantilla. The Braves had won, 1-0.

In his career, Henry never duplicated the blunder, which anyone might have made under the same circumstances. But it did get The Hammer into the record books under somewhat bizarre conditions.

Hank Aaron remained a remarkably consistent player throughout the 1960's as he inched closer to toppling the mightiest record of all.

Halfway through the decade, the Braves abandoned Milwaukee for Atlanta and Aaron, hoping to please the new fans quickly, determined to have a good initial year in the South in 1966. By June 30, he had hit 24 home runs to tie a

National League mark for homers hit in the first three months of the season. "As far as homers go, that's the hottest streak I've ever had," he recalled. He finished with 44 home runs and 127 runs batted in, leading the league in both departments and convincing the Atlanta fans they had the best player in baseball.

In 1969, three years after their Atlanta debut, the Braves won the western half of the National League pennant, thanks in large part to another 44 home runs by Aaron. That was the first season of divisional play, and the Braves had to meet the Eastern champs, the New York Mets, for a best-of-five championship series. Hank was ready. He homered in each of the first three games against the celebrated New York pitching staff, but the Braves, bedeviled by a leaky defense and sudden pitching collapse, lost all three, depriving Aaron of a chance to get into his third World Series.

Since that championship showing, the Braves haven't been a factor in the NL west, but that hasn't stopped Aaron. He slammed 38, 47, 34, and 40 homers in four succeeding seasons, although plagued by a series of minor ailments that in-cluded a damaged knee, a bad back and an arthritic neck. The knee was injured in a 1970 home plate collision with burly catcher Dick Dietz, then playing for the San Francisco Giants.

Montreal manager Gene Mauch, referring to Aaron's medical problems, says, "At one point, I didn't think he was going to catch Ruth. I didn't think he could over-come his injuries. But he takes care of himself and he's come back strong. I still feel that any pitch around the belt is next door to disaster."

Atlanta boss Eddie Mathews insists he never worried about the pressures Aaron would have to face.

"He's known the pressures of a black man breaking into baseball in the mid-1950s and he's experienced the pressures of stardom throughout his career," Mathews points out. "He hit .280 in 122 games as a rookie in 1954, lifted his average to .314 with 27 homers and 106 RBI in his sophomore season, and was the National League's batting champion with a .328 average in 1956. He's played in every All-Star Game since 1955, has hit more than .300 in 14 seasons, and has hit more than 35 homers in 11 seasons. These figures are cited to demonstrate that

Hank has spent his whole career in the limelight and is unlikely to encounter any pressures that he hasn't handled in the past."

It was in an All-Star Game that Henry Aaron felt the pressure more than he had ever felt it before. The setting was Detroit's Tiger Stadium in the summer of 1971.

"I think the most pressure I've ever felt was in the All-Star Game, at Detroit," recalls Aaron, who entered that game with a 10-for-57 All-Star record. "I'd never hit a home run in an All-Star Game up to then and I wanted desperately to hit a home run in that one because I didn't know if I'd get another chance to be in an All-Star Game."

Aaron got his wish, connecting with a Vida Blue delivery for his first All-Star homer. One year later, in the All-Star Game at Atlanta, Hank wished for another home run, hoping to please his hometown fans. He delivered again, hopping on a Gaylord Perry pitch with one man on base to put the Nationals ahead of the Americans for the moment by a 2-1 score.

The drama of the Atlanta All-Star homer was summed up best by Cincinnati's Joe Morgan, whose game-winning single won him the MVP trophy for the game. "When Aaron hit the homer, it was like watching a Hollywood movie. I thought he should be the hero."

Aaron nearly was. His shot off Perry had put the Nationals in front, but Cookie Rojas duplicated the feat, temporarily putting the AL in the lead, 3-2 before the NL tied it in the ninth. The press had already voted Aaron the game's MVP before a revote was taken after Morgan's game-winner in the 10th.

Several other milestone homers also came in pressure-packed situations for Aaron.

There was a one-week interval between No. 499 and No. 500, prompting Aaron to joke with Braves' president (now chairman) Bill Bartholomay, "I'm sorry you had to wait so long for it, Bill." And though Hank waited just two days between Nos. 599 and 600, the pitcher who served it up, Gaylord Perry, created some additional pressure beforehand, warning, "If Aaron gets it off me, he'll have to earn it."

There wasn't much time for the pressure to build for No. 700, even though only Ruth had reached that figure before Aaron did it July 21. The Atlanta star's conquest of the 700 figure came suddenly; he hit his 699th

Friday night, July 20, and the 700th the following evening.

One batting achievement which put considerable pressure on Aaron was his 3,000th hit, a goal he finally reached on May 17, 1970, at Cincinnati's old Crosley Field, which was to close by mid-season, when Riverfront Stadium was ready for occupancy by the Reds.

Aaron got the hit—an infield single—against Wayne Simpson, a righthander who then had a blazing fastball. The blow made Hank the sole occupant of the 3,000 hit/500 homer club until Willie Mays joined him two months later.

The Braves' star had hoped to hit a homer for his 3,000th, and the Atlanta equipment manager, Mark Gladulich, anticipating just that, stationed himself outside the park in the hope of retrieving it. Had the ball gone into the stands, traveling secretary Don Davidson was prepared to pay $200 to a fan in exchange for the ball. But then Aaron got his infield hit.

Most observers felt Henry would get his big hit in the opener of that Sunday doubleheader, but lefthander Jim Merritt set him down hitless in four tries in that game. "Merritt just outsmarted me," said Aaron when asked if he had been overanxious. "I would look for one pitch and he would throw another."

As for Simpson, Aaron said, "I hadn't seen him. I was just looking for the hard stuff."

After the milestone safety, Stan Musial, the last man to register that many hits (in 1958), and Braves' president Bill Bartholomay jumped onto the field to offer their congratulations.

When Aaron came up for his next at-bat, he homered, just as Musial did for his 3,001st hit.

"I'm glad it's finally over," Aaron said after the game. "I haven't had much rest since I got to within five hits of 3,000."

Three-thousand hits . . . a lofty achievement, and one never reached by Babe Ruth. Henry Aaron has reached one of his most important objectives on the road to baseball immortality.

It would seem the pressure applied by the media and by the lore of Babe Ruth would rattle Aaron, but that is hardly the case, according to Eddie Mathews. "He's accepted his super-star status better than anyone else I've ever seen," said Mathews, who was a super-star in his own right during his long career in the National League. "Hank is a great help to me as a manager. He's quiet, but he leads by example. He follows all the rules and never takes advantage of his position. Aaron's presence in the lineup is important. Look at all the home runs Darrell Evans hit. Evans is a good hitter, but having Hank behind him in the order gives him an edge. Pitchers can't pitch around Evans with Hank coming up next.

"Sure there's pressure from the media, but don't forget, Henry's been in the limelight for a long time and he's used to it. As far as the letters go, there will always be some people living in the past. Hank was exposed to his share of racial slurs early in his career and it upset him then. But now he has to forget it, at least to live with it, because it's always going to happen to some degree."

Darrell Evans also knows Aaron is under heavy pressure. "It's mentally tough on Hank because of all the demands on his time," says the powerful Atlanta third baseman. "But he's the kind of individual who can handle it. He's always on an even keel and never gets upset."

Willie Mays, who lived with the intense pressure of dealing with the aggressive New York press contingent on a daily basis, sympathizes with Aaron. "Hank is going through so much trying to explain on what day he will hit the home run and what day he is going to play," says Mays, who retired after the 1973 season. "It's just a little hard on him."

But Aaron remains unshaken, almost appearing as if he were under the influence of sedation in the eye of a storm. "It's no pressure on me, really," he said. "I feel like I have a job to do and I'm going out there and do it. My main purpose for being out here is to try and win ball games and help the Atlanta Braves. If it means trying to hit the ball to rightfield, then this is what I have to do. Remember, I haven't just started hitting home runs. I've been doing it for nineteen years. It's just recently that I started getting all this publicity."

Braves' medical consultant Dr. Robert Wells says Aaron is physically capable of taking the pressure, which must exist to a degree despite Henry's denials. "He looks at least six or seven years younger than he is," says the doctor "He is a strong, vigorous man, From a medical standpoint, he's one of the lesser problems on the Braves. I expect he will have recurrent minor medical

In the batter's box, Hank Aaron is a picture of intense concentration.

problems, but I don't foresee anything major. Also, let me point out that he's extremely stable emotionally. This helps."

Aaron insisted that his challenge to Ruth should not be compared to Roger Maris' 1961 feat of hitting 61 home runs in a single season, one more than Ruth achieved in his peak campaign of 1927. Maris had a time limit, Aaron pointed out, while he does not.

The Braves' star enjoys hearing the cheers of fans in batting practice, he admits, but doesn't hear anything when he's at bat during a game. At that point, everything else is blacked out and the only important thing is the one-to-one battle of Aaron against the pitcher.

"It makes you feel good during batting practice when you can walk into the cage and hit two or three balls out of the park and the fans stand up and cheer for you," says Aaron, whose popularity in Canada rivals that of the greatest Canadian sports heroes. "It makes you feel wanted, like everybody's pulling for you. And there are an awful lot of people in my corner who want to see me break the record.

"But once I step into that batter's box, I immediately start concentrating on the opposing pitcher. I've always been able to block things out of my mind, just to think in terms of baseball.

"It may sound silly, but I don't hear a thing when I'm up at bat. Someone can be standing and hollering right by the dugout, but I don't hear it. I'm concentrating on the pitcher. I don't worry about what's happening in the stands."

Aaron said he found an easy way to dissolve the pressure of his 700th home run: he simply went out and hit it.

"This was a historic moment because I would have been the second man to hit seven hundred home runs," he said. "There were cameras and newspapermen from all over. When I was a couple of home runs away, one of the guys on the team said to me 'How do you plan on getting all the pressure off you?' And I said, 'There's only one way to do it—go out and hit and they'll all disappear.' So that's what I did."

The barrage of hate mail he received did bother Aaron somewhat, but the wiry slugger merely redoubled his efforts to break the record that some regarded as too sacred to be reached by a black man.

When the Braves played in Chicago at one point midway through the 1973 season, Aaron visited a group of black Little Leaguers at the invitation of the Rev. Jesse Jackson, noted black activist, and read one of the hate letters to his audience.

In part, it read, "Why are they making such a big fuss about you hitting 700 home runs? Please remember that you have been to bat 2,700 more times than Babe Ruth. If Babe Ruth was at bat 2,700 more times, he would have hit 814 home runs. So, Hank, what are you bragging about? Let's have the truth. You mention that if you were white, they would give you more credit. That's ignorant, stupid. Hank, there's three things you can't give a nigger—a black eye, a puffed lip, or a job. . ."

Aaron branded it one of the "nicer" hate letters, then told his audience: "Things like this really make me push just that much harder. People just can't picture the idea that a black man could come into sports and break such a prodigious record that has been held so long by a white man. They just don't relish the idea that a black man is coming along and taking away some of the glory. I realized while growing up in Mobile that being a black person I already had two strikes against me and I certainly wasn't going to let them get the third strike. I felt like being a baseball player. I had one way to go—and that was up."

Even though pitchers swear he is superhuman at the plate, Aaron is a very sensitive and thoughtful human being. He had to be bothered by letters that began "Dear Nigger" or threatened the physical well-being of his family.

"All of this has just made me more determined to go out and break the record," he says. "I'm not out to destroy a record but to hit 715 or 770 home runs, or what have you, because I honestly believe records are made to be broken. I just hope that 10 or 15 years from now some kid will come along—whether he is black or white—and challenge my record. I'll certainly be pulling for him."

Aaron, a thoughtful, quiet man, generally keeps to himself, even among his teammates. If the pressure does bother him, he doesn't let it show. Mike Lum, who played first base and the outfield for the 1973 Braves, explains: "He's basically a shy person, a loner. He lets his bat do the talking for him and this is what he's been doing all of his career."

Yet Aaron, like anyone else, occasionally gets angry. To him, a man in the public eye, a man who daily risks his life by standing in the firing line of a tiny ball thrown with great velocity, the pressure can sometimes exceed the normal limits.

At least once since the Braves moved to Atlanta in 1966 Hank Aaron has exploded. There was a mid-air fight on the Braves' plane with teammate Rico Carty, a hot-tempered former boxer who allegedly aroused Aaron's ire with a racist remark.

Aaron gave this account of the incident to Ralph Blumenfeld of The New York Post: "We were in the back of the plane. Rico started talking about me in Spanish, but I knew it was about me. So I started kidding with Mike de la Hoz—and Rico thought I was talking about

him. He told me, 'Go to hell.' I told him, 'Go to hell yourself.' Then he called me a name."

Don Davidson says that only two punches were thrown before the two outfielders were separated.

"I'm sorry it happened," Hank said afterward. "But if anybody calls me that again, there'll be another fight. I don't go around calling people names and I'm not going to just stand there when somebody calls me that name."

What was the name? Apparently it implied unkind things about Aaron's mother in addition to having racial connotations. It seemed odd that Carty, whose complexion is darker than Aaron's, would hurl racial insults against another black man, but observers of the incident swear that's what happened.

One witness said that Carty flew into a rage when Aaron answered his racial slur with the line, "Well, you're not exactly pink yourself." It is conceivable that Hank did say it, trying to remain cool under the pressure of the moment and stave off a confrontation. Other witnesses say it never happened.

The Braves kept Carty several more seasons after the 1967 airplane brawl, but he and Aaron were distant.

Rico Carty and Aaron traded punches after name-calling incident in airplane.

After the 1972 season, Rico finally left the Braves after his trade to the Texas Rangers.

The present pressures on Aaron, however, seem to have blocked out the unpleasant incidents of the past. The Hammer is finally getting the recognition—and even the endorsements—he was denied for so long. In fact, it sometimes seems as if the newsmen and advertising agencies are trying to make up for all the years they missed, the years when Aaron was racing toward the record at full throttle while the newsmen and advertisers were chasing Mickey Mantle and Willie Mays.

Today Aaron can laugh at the pressure. On the night he hit his 713th home run, a writer reminded him that he could pass Babe Ruth in lifetime runs batted in during the 1974 season. "Oh, here we go with Babe Ruth again," he laughed. "I thought once I passed him in home runs all the other records would be gone automatically. What other records did he have?"

The Atlanta star can also look at his situation realistically. "I think I've slowed down," he said near the end of the 1973 season. "You notice it most after a hard night game, especially when you have to go 12 innings or so, where you have to make a lot of putouts and throws.

"You notice it at the plate sometimes when you foul off pitches you should have hit out. In the field, some balls I should have caught dropped in. And sometimes going from first to third I got tired. Baseball is a young man's game. When you reach 35 or 36 and you're still having good seasons, you're really fortunate."

National League pitchers don't think Henry's reflexes or wrist action are any slower today than they were five or six years ago, and the batting statistics don't reveal it either, with the single exception of that .265 average in 1972. But even that career-low average can be explained away because of the spring player strike that set back many veterans, including Aaron, and because of the infield shifts pulled by other teams when Aaron came to bat.

The pressure figures to be heavy on NL pitchers every time Aaron comes up from now until his retirement simply because every home run he hits after his first one of the 1974 season will be a new standard in that department.

Tom Seaver, regarded as the NL's standout pitcher, admitted he still regards Aaron with the utmost respect. "He's just as strong now as when I came up in 1967—no question," says the star righthander. "He's always taken very good care of himself physically. He keeps himself in great shape and he's a superb athlete.

"I think I've been around long enough to know that Henry is one of the best hitters in the league. I pitch to him the same way I would pitch to anybody else in certain situations. I have a way that I do pitch to him, depending on men-on-base, score, and so on. He's obviously the one guy on that club you don't want to beat you. But you can't pitch to

him with The Record in mind. You take it as it comes."

Steve Blass, another righthander, also talks about Aaron and the record. "When I was a kid, I thought that was a pretty safe record," he says. "But I don't feel it's sacred. If we went along on that premise, we'd say all records are sacred and they shouldn't be broken. Then there wouldn't be much of a game left. So he's more than justified in trying to break the record.

"I just think of how many home runs Aaron has hit off me and how tough a hitter he is to pitch against," Blass continues. "He's very menacing up there. It's tough for me to be able to throw the kind of pitches I want because I know what kind of power he has and how capable he is of hitting it out of the ballpark."

Blass says he likes to throw Aaron sliders away from the plate. "But every once in awhile, I have to come in because if you try pitching against him one way consistently, he'll adjust very quickly."

Claude Osteen, who gave up two Aaron homers in 1965, 1967, and 1968, three in 1969, and four in 1971, explains: "If you pitch regularly every year—every fourth or fifth day—he's bound to hit some off you. You just take it as it comes. He hits one out, then you forget about it and work on the next hitter."

A veteran San Francisco pitcher says, "Name the way you'd like to get beat and Aaron will beat you. You don't see Henry's fire but you feel it. It rubs off on everybody around."

Aaron rates Tom Seaver, Bob Gibson, Juan Marichal, Don Drysdale, and Sandy Koufax as among the toughest pitchers he has faced during his 20 big-league seasons, but insists that—for him—Curt Simmons was the most difficult of all.

"Over the years, Curt Simmons was the toughest," says Aaron of the lefthander who performed with the Phillies and Cardinals. "Even though I had trouble with Curt, things usually even out in baseball. One year, a pitcher can give you a lot of trouble but the next year you catch up with him. But Simmons gave me the most problems."

Simmons also gave Aaron a pitch which resulted in the most controversial home run of his career. In fact, it isn't even counted among Hank's total of 713 heading into the 1974 season.

Bob Uecker, an old Aaron teammate then catching for St. Louis, was behind the plate and Chris Pelekoudas was the umpire when the incident occurred. Simmons made his delivery, Aaron swung, and the ball disappeared into the leftfield stand at old Busch Stadium. Uecker and Simmons protested and Pelekoudas called the startled Aaron back to the batter's box. Simmons and Uecker had complained that, at the moment Aaron hit the ball, his left (front) foot was out of the batter's box.

"I never held it against Chris because he felt he was making the right decision," says Aaron. "I can't criticize his judgment. He's the umpire and I'm still looking for 714, so he must have made the right decision."

Despite his uncanny ability to handle Aaron, Simmons, long retired from the game, remembers, "Trying to throw a fastball by Hank Aaron is like trying to sneak the sun past a rooster."

Pat Jarvis, a former teammate, says of Aaron, "He's always looking for the fastball and usually hits it. I wouldn't try to throw my fastball by him, because nobody can."

Aaron's ability to hit a fastball at age 40 is as essential to his success as his relaxed attitude, especially when it comes to fighting the pressures of winning ball games and breaking records.

"Things do bother me," he admits, "but I react differently than other people. Some guys go 0-for-4 and throw their helmets or kick things. But I think 'Why did I pop up? Why did I strike out?' This is how I try to teach my kids . . . to sit down and figure things out. I'm never satisfied, really. I always feel there's room for improvement. If I hit two homers, I wonder why I didn't hit three. But I know you can't be as good as the other guy every day."

Rival managers realize every home run Aaron hits increases his appetite. Cincinnati's Spanky Anderson ordered Aaron purposely passed in a game last year with two outs and a man on third in the bottom of the eighth. "I'm not going to let Hank Aaron beat me in that situation," he said. "I wouldn't care if he had retired and came down out of the stands to hit. He lives for those kind of situations."

Walt Alston of the Dodgers, dean of major league managers, entered the managerial end of baseball in 1954, the same season Aaron made the majors. He's oc-casionally walked Aaron intentionally even though the Braves' star represented the game's winning run. "I know there just isn't any way to pitch to him," Alston said.

Montreal's Gene Mauch, second in managerial longevity to Alston, says, "We feel the same way about him today we did 15 years ago. He's a very dangerous hit- . ter."

The pressure is on Aaron, but it's also on his opponents—and that helps.

After Aaron crashed his 600th homer off Gaylord Perry early in the 1971 season, Willie Mays made a startling prediction. "He's not through rocking this place yet," said the veteran outfielder of Aaron, whose homer had sent Atlanta Stadium's fans into a frenzy. "If you think the fans got shook up tonight, tell 'em to just stick around."

At fighting the pressure and hitting home runs, Hank Aaron is the undisputed king. In pursuing the ghost and the legend of Babe Ruth, the mild-mannered Atlanta star has met challenges Ruth could not have dreamed of.

When he breaks the record during the early part of the 1974 season, Henry Aaron will have climbed the greatest mountain in baseball history. ●

The two faces of a baseball legend: Babe Ruth (L) and Henry Aaron.

THE BABE
AND THE HAMMER

■ Hank Aaron took on more than a record when he set out to challenge Babe Ruth's mark of 714 lifetime home runs; he took on a legend, a myth that endures 26 years after Ruth's death.

"There has always been a magic about that gross, ugly, coarse, Gargantuan figure of a man and everything he did," wrote Paul Gallico of Ruth.

In his quiet, conservative way, Henry Aaron is not trying to challenge that magic, but merely attempting to set a new home run standard which, quite possibly, will never be equaled.

The contrast between the

two men is remarkable, as is the contrast between the game of baseball that Ruth played and the game as it is structured today.

The most amazing coincidence about the two men is that their birthdays are just one day apart. Aaron was born on Feb. 5, 1934, and Ruth on Feb. 6, 1895, making both men Aquarians. Aaron is a black man from Mobile, Alabama; Ruth was a white man from Baltimore, Maryland.

Both came into great wealth in baseball after emerging from poverty, both spent little time in the minor leagues, both were consistent performers in the majors, and both spent the better part of their careers as rightfielders. In addition, both were paid as well as the Presidents who saw them play.

When Ruth held out for an $80,000 contract in the spring of 1930, a writer pointed out that President Hoover made only $75,000 in that Depression year.

"Yeah," snapped Ruth, "but I had a better year than he did."

Hank Aaron had a better year than President Richard Nixon in 1973, but did not have to renegotiate his three-year contract, which runs through the 1974 season and calls for $200,000 a season, the same salary the President receives. When he signed it prior to the 1972 season, Aaron admitted, "The contract is for more than one year, more than two years, enough time to go after Ruth's record." He made it clear that the three-year contract would be his last as a player. "After twenty years, I'm sick of traveling," he said.

Ruth did not have to make the tiring cross-country trips required of today's players. In his day, the westernmost outpost of the American League was St. Louis.

"One of the toughest things about playing these days is the travel," says Aaron. "When you make that swing out to the West Coast to play the Dodgers, Giants and Padres, your sleeping and eating habits get all messed up. I notice that certain pitchers give me trouble out there but I seem to be able to handle them back in our park."

Aaron, not the type who complains about anything, shrugs off the inevitable comparisons with Babe Ruth. "I can't comment on what Ruth faced," he states matter-of-factly. "But I really don't think pitching then was as tough as it is now. I'm not talking about four or five 20-

73

game winners. I'm thinking about pitchers who win 16-20 games every season. There are no patsies anymore. Every team has at least one and probably two good pitchers. You find them in San Diego, Philadelphia, and every other city. Pitching is not any better now than it was seven years ago, but today you see more good pitchers."

Aaron also must learn more pitchers than Ruth. There are now 11 opposing staffs for the Braves' star to study, against seven for Ruth when the Yankees played under the old eight-club format.

"I keep a mental book on what the pitchers throw me," explains Aaron, a study in modesty, self-discipline and physical conditioning. "When I'm hitting well, I can tell what a pitch will be when it's about halfway to the plate."

Because modern managers delight in parading an endless stream of relief pitchers with unorthodox deliveries and trick pitches, Henry has to keep track of rival pitchers and their assortments. Babe Ruth did not have to cope with the phenomenon of relief pitching as it exists today. Nor did he ever play night baseball, which was first played in 1935, the same year Ruth

Aaron signs lucrative contract as owner William Bartholomay watches.

retired from the game.

The improvement in pitching, emphasis on relief men, and advent of night baseball were the three prime factors which caused the over-all major league batting average to fall from .282 in Ruth's heyday to .252 today. That decline is reflected in Hank Aaron's lifetime batting average of .310, which can be favorably compared with Ruth's .342 when the 30-point differential is considered.

Aaron, realizing things have changed, often thinks about his challenge of Ruth's record. "You know, it's hard for me to believe I have a shot at it," he mused one night shortly after the 1973 All-Star Game. "It's just one of those things you sort of never even think about until one day you suddenly realize that here is something great that might be within your reach."

The National Broadcasting Company, which specializes in baseball with its Game of the Week, All-Star Game and World Series television coverage, also realized Aaron had a shot at Ruth's mark. The news-conscious network covered the countdown after the Atlanta slugger had whittled the difference between his total and Babe Ruth's to a number he could count on one hand.

NBC, interrupting its prime-time programming to show videotaped replays of Aaron home runs in late September, gave an audience of an estimated 30 million Americans a glimpse of instant history with the Aaron film clips. Certainly, Ruth's homers weren't covered live by camera crews, nor did the country realize the significance of 714 when it was recorded in 1935. What they did know was that Babe Ruth had made an immense contribution to the game of baseball and that he was one of the best—if not the best— players who ever lived.

Leo Durocher, asked about Ruth, reported, "The Babe never made a mistake. He never threw to the wrong base; he was a much better outfielder than you thought he was. He could run pretty well for a big man; he could do a lot of things."

The one-time field pilot of the Giants, Dodgers, Cubs and Astros also has high praise for Aaron's all-around ability. "When I first knew him, Aaron was a great hitter with great power and a fine outfielder with a good arm," recalls Durocher. "If he wanted to do it, he could steal a base like it wasn't there. A few years ago, when Aaron got on second base, if you didn't watch him, third base was his. When he left, he stole it. You **never** threw him out."

Speed is the main difference between Hank and the Babe on the field. Ruth did manage to steal 17 bases in two separate seasons early in his career, but never topped the 20 mark, which Aaron did on six separate occasions.

Both Aaron and Ruth were devastating power-hitters playing on teams laden with long-ball power. For most of Ruth's career, Lou Gehrig followed him in the lineup, forcing pitchers to give Ruth pitches around the plate. They were reluctant to walk

Babe and risk a two-run home run by Gehrig. Likewise, Aaron has always had a home run threat behind him.

"If the man hitting behind me has a good year," Hank says, "opposing pitchers can't pitch around me. They have to give me some pitches to hit. I've been fortunate throughout my career in having someone with power hitting behind me in the lineup—Eddie Mathews, Joe Adcock, Rico Carty, Orlando Cepeda, Earl Williams and Dusty Baker. I'm as good as the fellow hitting behind me."

Aaron, who bats right-handed, is a vastly different hitter than Ruth. He has an unorthodox swing and gets most of his power from his quick, powerful wrists. Ruth, on the other hand, was a lefthanded batter who was built like a pot-bellied stove. His massive shoulders and forearms contained the great strength which transformed itself from his arms to his bat.

One of the game's all-time home run stars, Ralph Kiner, analyzes Aaron's swing. "One of the things that makes him so great," says the former Pittsburgh star, now an announcer for the Mets, "is his ability to shift his weight as he hits the ball. You know, there is a theory of hitting that says you must not shift your weight forward, that you must keep the weight on your back foot at all times. Most hitters are taught this way, but I don't believe it's true. I believe that hitters do shift their weight forward—in fact, I don't believe they could hit if they didn't. Nowadays, we have slow-motion film and television tape that show this very clearly. But among many baseball people, the ideas persist that you must keep your weight back."

Eddie Mathews, who's observed Aaron at close range for most of his 20-year career, observes, "He developed his own style as a young player and has kept it throughout his career. He isn't a classic hitter and young players shouldn't try to copy him. He hits off the front foot—a flat-footed stance in any batting textbook. It would sound wrong to say that the man destined to break Ruth's career home run record has a fundamental flaw in his batting style. Let's just say that Hank Aaron hits differently than anyone else."

Aaron had an even more fundamental batting flaw before he was signed by the

A familiar scene in 1973—Aaron touching home plate after clouting home run.

Braves. "When I first started playing baseball, I held my hands the wrong way—I had them crossed over," he recalls. "I was playing with the Indianapolis Clowns, a barnstorming team, when scout Dewey Griggs came to watch me. He couldn't believe how I held the bat. But I hit .467 in the Negro American League that way.

"Anyway, Griggs told me, during a game, to hold the bat the right way. I tried it and got a hit. It felt comfortable that way too. After awhile, I wasn't comfortable in the cross-handed method. But all I had to do then was hold a bat that way and turn around and I could have hit lefty. Then I wouldn't have had so much trouble with righties like Drysdale, Gibson and Seaver."

Nonetheless, Hank earned such a reputation as a righthanded hitter that Ted Williams, a lefthanded batter whose big bat won him a niche in baseball's Hall of Fame, said of him, "He knows more about the pitchers in the National League than anyone playing today. He's a real student. He waits for his pitch and makes them throw it."

Ruth was also a student of hitting, primarily because he learned about the art from the pitcher's point of view.

The Babe came into pro ball as a fireballing lefthanded pitcher, finally making the majors with the 1914 Boston Red Sox after his contract was purchased from the old Baltimore Orioles of the I.L.

He was 2-1 that first year, then ran up successive records of 18-8, 23-12, and 24-13 as a full-time pitcher. His 1.75 ERA led the American League in 1916. But Ruth had shown so much ability with a bat that by 1918, he was playing the outfield on days he wasn't pitching.

In 1918, Ruth was 13-7 and had 11 home runs in 95 games. The following year, his last with the Red Sox, he was 9-5 as a pitcher, but had a .322 batting average, 29 homers, and 114 runs batted in as a hitter.

Ruth's career mark on the mound was 94 wins, 46 defeats, with a fine 2.28 earned run average. He was 3-0 with an 0.87 ERA in the World Series and for 43 years held the record for most consecutive scoreless innings pitched in the Fall Classic. He even pitched the final game of the 1933 season for the Yankees and—despite his ballooning proportions—staggered to a 6-5 complete game victory, smashing a home run in the process.

Aaron was not a pitcher at any stage of his career but, like Ruth, became a star after becoming a full-time right-fielder. Hank was signed as an infielder by the Braves and, although converted to the outfield in time for his big league debut in 1954, often filled in as an infielder when the Braves needed emergency help there, particularly at second base. Aaron, for example, played 27 games at second for the Braves in 1955 and 11 more in 1964.

The greatest controversy in the Aaron-Ruth comparison stems from the fact that Ruth collected his 714 home runs in 8,399 times at bat, nearly 3,000 fewer than Aaron, who had 11,228 heading into the 1974 season. Ruth ranks first in the number of home runs per 100 times at bat over the course of his career with 8.5.

Many pro-Ruth fans feel Commissioner Bowie Kuhn should follow the precedent set by former Commissioner Ford Frick, who put an asterisk (*) next to Roger Maris' single-season record of 61 homers in 1961, because Maris accomplished the feat in a 162-game schedule while Ruth had set the original mark of 60 under the old 154-game format.

Mrs. Babe Ruth hinted she would like the idea when she said "Hank Aaron is setting a record of his own for someone else to shoot at. As far as I'm concerned, there was only one Babe and he stands alone."

Aaron himself says, "I don't really care what they say about times at bat. I've got 3,300 or 3,400 hits, too, and Ruth didn't get that."

Though Braves' coach Connie Ryan maintains that, "Henry Aaron is the type of player who would fit into any era," Ruth's fans persist in their argument that Aaron's additional batting appearances have dulled the shine on the home run crown he'll inherit in 1974.

A pro-Ruth fan actually calculated that adding the 2,800 at-bats to Ruth's career could have given him an additional 231 home runs at the same ratio, or a career total of 945! The same fan suggested that record-keepers deduct five per cent of that achievement because of the home run advantage accorded a lefthanded hitter. He came out with a new total of 898 home runs, and suggested that Aaron not be regarded as the new home run king until he passed that figure! Obviously, the Braves' slugger will fall far short of that goal.

The advantage for a lefty is

suggested in the fact that there are far more righthanded than lefthanded pitchers in baseball, and a lefthander has a statistical edge batting against a righthander just as a righthander has an edge batting against a southpaw. The reason is that a righthanded pitcher throws a ball that tends to move away from a righthanded hitter, while a lefthander's ball generally moves toward a righthanded batter's power zone.

Being lefthanded certainly helped Ruth account for quite a number of his home runs. After leaving the Red Sox to join the Yankees in 1920, he had the good fortune to play in the old Polo Grounds because Yankee Stadium had not yet been built. The ballpark, also the home of the New York Giants, was made for a left-handed hitter, the right-field fence was just 254 feet from home plate. It was an easy mark for the Babe, who smashed 54 home runs that season, 25 more than he hit in 1919, although his 29 that season set an all-time record. Ruth again broke his own mark with 59 in 1921, then slipped to 35 in 1922 when he spent a third of the season under suspension by his own team.

In 1923, Yankee Stadium opened and was instantly given a suitable subtitle by the press: "The House That Ruth Built." It wasn't called that without good reason. The friendly rightfield porch, though deeper than the Polo Grounds in that corner, was still just 296 feet away, one of the easiest targets in the game.

Ruth didn't waste any time finding it. He hit 41 homers that first year and, by 1927, had adjusted so well that he broke his own record by hitting 60 in a single season. In his peak, from 1926 through 1932, Ruth never hit less than .323 or had fewer than 41 homers in a season.

Aaron, too, played in parks conducive to the long ball, first at Milwaukee Stadium and later in Atlanta Stadium. The air is thin in the Georgia capital and balls hit hard and up usually find their way over the fence.

Both Ruth and Aaron have critics who contend that their achievements were tainted by easy ballparks, but that argument is fruitless because it would negate the meaning of all baseball records. Every stadium is different. What if Ted Williams, a lefthanded batter, had played his home games at Yankee Stadium or if the righthanded Harmon

Aaron gets most of his home run power from his quick, powerful wrist action.

Batting lefthanded at Polo Grounds and Yankee Stadium gave Ruth an edge.

Killebrew had played his at cozy Fenway Park in Boston? Would they be the all-time home run kings? The debate seems endless.

The changing conditions of the game seem more significant in deciding who should wear the home run crown. In addition to the longer schedule, increased travel, emphasis on night ball, two expansions, and the general improvement in pitching, Aaron also faced other problems not encountered by Ruth.

One, of course, was the challenge of breaking another man's record. Another was the pressure of constant exposure in the media. Radio began in 1920, when Ruth was in his seventh season in the majors. Television did not come into its own until after World War II. Also, because Aaron did not enjoy the explosive home run seasons of Ruth, who hit 54 or more homers in a season four different times, it was important for the modern star to remain in good physical condition in the latter years of his career. It's tough to keep an athletic figure when a man approaches age 40.

"My health is my main thought at this time," said Aaron midway through the 1973 season. "In my mind, a hitter is always able to hit, but first he must be fit and able to get on the field to play. Thankfully I am in good health and my knee—which bothered me some in the past—is fine," continued the svelte slugger, who has added less than 10 pounds to the 6-foot, 180-pound frame he carried when he first appeared in the Braves' spring training camp in 1954.

In his prime, Ruth was 6-2 and 235 pounds, but he was much heavier by the time he closed out his career in the mid-1930s. His record reflected the fact that Babe was out of shape. After hitting 41 homers at age 37 in 1932, he slipped to 34 at 38, 22 at 39, and finally—after being released by the Yankees and signed by the Boston Braves—just six in 1935 at age 40. His last three home runs came on May 25 at Pittsburgh's spacious old park, Forbes Field. By Memorial Day, Ruth, realizing he was through, quit baseball.

The rotund Yankee slugger was felled by his own insatiable appetite for life's pleasures. Even at age 30, Ruth had physical problems. At that age, in 1925, Ruth guzzled countless hot dogs, sodas, and beers during spring training and triggered a gastric revolt by his overtaxed digestive tract. He was limited to just 98 games that season, but still managed to swat 25 homers, a tribute to his sharp batting eye, excellent coordination and brute strength.

Ruth's teammate and friend, Waite Hoyt, used to joke that if someone sawed the Babe in two, half the concessions of Yankee Stadium would fall out.

One of the Babe's favorite culinary delights was a concoction of chocolate ice cream and pickled eels prepared by Lou Gehrig's mother. He used to devour this delicacy (?) between games of doubleheaders at the Stadium. Ruth's appetite was so huge that he regularly consumed a mammoth breakfast to start the day. On a train trip one morning, he downed a pint of bourbon and ginger ale, a porterhouse steak, four fried eggs, fried potatoes and a pot of coffee.

Ruth also enjoyed himself after dark, when he would unwind from the day's action at the ballpark.

Once, Washington's Goose Goslin tried to tire Ruth for the next day's game by keeping him out late the night before. The two men enjoyed themselves until sun-up, when Goslin returned to his hotel room, hoping to recuperate in time

Ex-batting great Ralph Kiner says weight shift is key to Aaron's hitting ability.

for that afternoon's game. Ruth went straight to Walter Reed Hospital to autograph balls and visit the sick. In the game, Goslin went 0-for-5 while Ruth hit two home runs and a double.

Obviously, Ruth's career record might have been far greater had he observed training rules and maintained his physical condition.

"He had to be the greatest power-hitter, the greatest player," said Stan Musial of Ruth. "He was good enough to pitch and bat fourth, like the star of a high school team."

A young fan once asked Ruth if he could hit .400 by concentrating on his average instead of the long ball. Babe replied, "Four hundred, hell. I could have hit five hundred!"

Modesty was not one of Ruth's virtues, though it is one of the strong points of Hank Aaron's personality. Of Babe Ruth, Aaron insists, "He'll still be the best, even if I pass him. Babe Ruth will still be regarded as the greatest home run hitter who ever lived."

Ruth, unlike Aaron, was not a serious, thoughtful man. "Babe was a loveable, big-hearted fellow," said Harry Hooper, the man who convinced Boston Red Sox manager Ed Barrow to convert Ruth to the outfield.

"He had his weaknesses. On the train, we'd send out for a sandwich and a soda pop. Babe would send out for half-a-dozen sandwiches and half-a-dozen soda pops. Just about ruined his stomach.

"He had a big belly, but it didn't hurt his hitting."

Once, hurt by insults against his intellect, Ruth challenged a sportswriter to ask him a question relating to classical literature. "I am a serious guy," Ruth told the writer. "I read books."

The writer, seizing the opportunity, responded, "What do you think of the Napoleonic Era?"

Ruth answered, "I think it should have been scored a hit."

By contrast, Aaron is a serious thinker who is very aware that, as a black man, he represents the hopes of millions of black kids who, 30 years ago, could not even think about playing major league baseball.

"He has begun reading books by and about Dr. Martin Luther King in the past few months and we often talk about black affairs," said the future Mrs. Aaron, Billye Williams, as the 1973 baseball season entered its final month.

Aaron himself observed, "Many times, we black athletes haven't spoken out.

Aaron connecting for 693rd homer off Al Downing in Atlanta Stadium.

I've been guilty myself. But I've learned that when you don't say anything, people think you are satisfied. I'm not talking about being violent or militant. I'm talking about standing up for what's right. Now, because of the situation I'm in, I hope I can inspire a few kids to be a success in life. I want to break Ruth's record as an example to children, especially black children."

The veteran outfielder added, "When you speak your piece and it doesn't go anyplace, then you just wait until the right time. When I had four hundred home runs, nobody listened to Henry Aaron. I thought, 'I'm just going to wait.'

"When I began to challenge Ruth's record, then everybody wanted to listen and see what Henry Aaron has to say. I've always spoken out on issues about things that pertained to black and white. I've always felt I had to be my own man and look in the mirror and face these things."

His black awareness recently included hosting a 1972 winter bowling tournament that raised $25,000 to help fight sickle cell anemia, a disease that strikes blacks. Also, he has worked closely with the Rev. Jesse Jackson of Chicago and the Rev. Leon Sullivan, author of the Philadelphia Plan, a black self-help program.

Ironically, as a boy, Hank Aaron knew little of Babe Ruth. "Why should I have read about a man playing a game I couldn't get into at the time?" he says today.

For both Aaron and Ruth, baseball was everything. The game gave both men a chance to escape from the poverty of their youth. But, when it mattered most to Ruth, baseball let him down. He felt he had done something for the game and the game should do something for him. Many Americans agreed with him.

Ruth was downcast and dejected when he failed to receive a major-league manager's job after his playing career had ended.

But the owners who might have considered him felt that he was ill-qualified to handle 25 players because he could hardly handle himself during his tempestuous—though successful—career. They remembered the string of violations and suspensions capped by a $5,000 fine assessed by Yankee Manager Miller Huggins in 1925.

Aaron is exactly the opposite. He has never been a problem to any of his managers in the majors and would certainly be considered for a field manager's job himself if he had shown an interest in such a position. Chances are good he will get his chance to prove his baseball savvy in a front office capacity once his playing days end.

Aaron could be the first black general manager after he retires. To date, the sure-fire future Hall of Famer has been outspoken in his criticism of the baseball establishment for not hiring blacks as field managers or general managers.

"If a black player is talented enough on the field to draw $100,000 or $150,000 a year for three or four years, he can offer some ballclub experience in the front office or coaching or managing jobs," says Aaron, whose brother Tommie became the highest-ranking black manager ever in 1973 when he was named pilot of the Double-A Savannah Braves.

"Don't just exploit someone's talents on the

field and not take advantage of his talents in the front office," says The Hammer. "On the field, blacks have been able to be super giants. But once our playing days are over, this is the end of it and we go back to the back of the bus again."

Aaron emphasized the point when he concluded, "The only stride the black player has made is in salaries. We have been able to get some of the high salaries but that's it. We haven't been able to break the ice in any of the other areas. Nothing has changed for blacks as far as managers, front-office personnel, and coaching positions in the 20 years I've been playing."

According to those who know him, Aaron would be an ideal man to break baseball's tradition of whites-only in managerial and executive spots (though Atlanta farm director Bill Lucas, Aaron's former brother-in-law, is black). Aaron himself suggested, "I think I could build a winning ballclub."

Earl Williams, the erudite Baltimore Orioles slugger and former member of the Braves, said of Aaron, "He has a vast knowledge of baseball and situations governing the inner workings of the game. These are things that people don't realize.

Hank could be good at whatever he decided to do. If he decided to be a manager, he'd be a good one.

"He carries himself well and has a lot of class. He is a quiet, soft-spoken guy, but not to the point of being mute. When he speaks, he doesn't waste his time with trivialities. He speaks what is on his mind and it's usually something very relevant and important."

Aaron's low-key style contrasts sharply with the bombastic image of Ruth, a big man who lived his life—on and off the field—in a big way. In the words of Leo Durocher, "Babe Ruth had charisma. When he walked into the locker room, you knew it."

Aaron, on the other hand, went almost unnoticed before the 1973 countdown began. The Braves' slugger preferred it that way. Often, he doesn't say a word to his teammates on buses or planes. Clete Boyer, who finished his major league career with the Braves, once said of him, "I'd rather drink alone than go out with Aaron. That man just isn't fun."

Of course, that's not the image Aaron's family has of him, but his family life is basically a private affair. Among the things that are known about Aaron is that he

Ex-batting great Ted Williams calls Aaron a real "student" of hitting.

into the stands by that quick snap of the wrists. Ruth, on the other hand, had a powerful, graceful swing with a smoother arc. His home runs followed great, sweeping curves en route to their final destinations far beyond the outfield fences.

Those who saw him play say Ruth's home runs were majestic shots which earned him the nickname "the Sultan of Swat." Likewise, Aaron's straight-to-the-point home runs have earned him his nickname of "The Hammer," a shortened version of "Hamerin' Hank," a name originally coined by Don Davidson, the team's traveling secretary and the only person besides Aaron who has seen 712 of Hank's homers. Davidson missed only one.

Those who knew him remember Ruth as a larger-than-life character, a real man who might just as easily have been the star of a cartoon strip.

Ruth is credited with saving the game of baseball following the 1919 Black Sox scandal, the most severe threat to the game in its colorful 105-year history. His camel-hair coat, snappy roadster, ever-present cigar, and infectious smile were almost as widely known as the graceful lefthanded

drives a Chevrolet Caprice, contradicting the adage that home run hitters drive Cadillacs. "It gets me around," he explains.

Aaron's swing gets him around on the diamond. "He swings his bat faster than anyone else in the game," explains Dodger batting coach Dixie Walker, who observes other hitters as well as his own. "At the explosion point where the bat meets the ball, Henry's bat packs the power it does because of the speed he gives it with that whiplash of his wrists."

His specialty is line-drive homers, propelled quickly

Pete Rose (L) says, "The Babe was great . . . but so is Henry Aaron!"

swing that powered balls far beyond outfield barriers.

He was a man with the heart of a little boy. He indulged autograph-seekers for hours and went out of his way to make people feel good, no matter who they were.

Once, when he met President Calvin Coolidge before a game in Washington, Ruth's friendly but crude nature overcame him. "Geez, it's hot, ain't it, Prez?" he said. Ruth's own teammates referred to him openly as The Big Monkey and The Big Baboon, names he didn't like but which stuck anyway.

The name Babe Ruth was so synonymous with America that during World War II—which began for the U.S. in 1941, six years after Ruth's retirement—Japanese troops goaded American GIs with shouts of "To hell with Babe Ruth!"

Some of Ruth's old fans are now saying "To hell with Hank Aaron," whom they regard as an upstart challenger with inferior credentials. They insist he did not hit the tape-measure shots of Ruth, who set long-distance records at Forbes Field and other parks with far-removed fences.

Yet they fail to realize the myriad of obstacles Aaron has overcome en route to the all-time home run crown. Today, relief specialists are trained in the minors; in Ruth's day it was not only an insult to be assigned to the bullpen, but starters stayed in far longer than they do today. Recapping further:

• Only big-city papers covered baseball on a daily basis in the Roaring Twenties, while today reporters from all over the country and even some from foreign countries are covering Aaron's exploits.

The pressure of the mass media is far more significant today. Radio was in its infancy and television unheard of in Ruth's heyday.

• Aaron plays most of his games at night, when it is much more difficult to see the baseball. Ruth never played a night game because he retired in May 1935, the same month the first night contest was played in Cincinnati.

• Ruth was the principal beneficiary of baseball's switch to the lively ball in 1920, whereas the home run as an offensive weapon was firmly established when Hank Aaron broke in, making his perennial long-ball achievements seem less significant.

• Ruth, as a lefthand hitter, had the twin advantages of the short rightfield fences at the Polo Grounds (254 feet) and later at Yankee Stadium (296) plus the good fortune to face primarily righthanded pitchers simply because there are more righties than lefties. Aaron, a righthanded batter, did not have the advantage of facing primarily lefthanders and had to aim at outfield fences of 320 feet down the leftfield line in Milwaukee and 330 in Atlanta.

• The Babe also had the advantage of having Lou Gehrig bat behind him in the Yankee lineup. Although Aaron also had home run threats following him, none could compare with Gehrig, whose presence frightened pitchers into giving Ruth better pitches to hit.

• Most important in the Ruth-Aaron controversy is the fact that Aaron has the extreme disadvantage of chasing another man's record. That fact alone puts pressure on the Atlanta star. When Ruth was collecting his

Eddie Mathews, now Atlanta manager, was another who hit behind Hank in lineup.

714 home runs, he had no definite goal in mind and no pressure. It just so happened that he reached that figure before realizing he couldn't play baseball any longer.

Aaron is reminded of the countdown every time he comes to bat. The umpire halts the game to throw in a new set of balls specially marked with invisible ink for identification purposes in the event he should hit one of them over the fence. To fans who believe the umpires are assisting Aaron by using these new balls, there are two facts to bear in mind: (1) they are good old American balls, not the new souped-up Haitian balls which were the center of a brief controversy in 1973, and (2) the use of the special "Aaron ball" makes the pitcher bear down even harder. Fans who think pitchers "gave" Aaron easy pitches because the Braves were out of contention in 1973 are wrong.

Pitchers are a proud bunch who use their earned run averages as indicators of success when negotiating their contracts; no NL pitcher wants to blow his chance for a raise because he "gave" Hank Aaron—or anyone else—a home run pitch.

Right through the 1973 season, Hank Aaron, playing down his achievement, insisted, "It's hard to compare Ruth's record with anything because the structure of baseball has changed so much since that time. We play in Atlanta one day and then fly to Los Angeles. This has to take something out of a baseball player's career."

Aaron also reminds his fans, "I am not always thinking home run when I step to the plate. I am concentrating on getting a hit, trying to win the game. If a home run is needed, **then** I think it is my duty to try and get it. First you play baseball, then you play to win, and then you go for home runs. The understanding of the fans is important."

Pete Rose, the star Cincinnati outfielder who has a slight edge on Aaron for the highest lifetime average in the National League, is a great admirer of Hank's. Of the race with Ruth, Rose says, "I feel like I know the Babe. He was great, but so is Aaron."

That's probably the way the baseball histories will record the two men—two immortals with vastly different styles and personalities playing in vastly different eras while recording slugging records that will stand forever. •

FROM MOBILE TO MILWAUKEE

■ Henry Louis Aaron was the third child of eight born to Herbert and Estella Aaron of Mobile, Ala. He was born on Feb. 5, 1934, when Mobile was in the grip of the Great Depression and no blacks were in baseball's major leagues.

There was little to do in Mobile but fish and play ball. Aaron played football for Central High School, one of the town's segregated schools which did not have a baseball team. He was a good halfback and end—and was even offered a college football scholarship at one point—but his first love was baseball.

"He used to play by himself in the backyard for hours," recalls his mother, who once disciplined young Henry for transforming her new mop into a stickball bat. "He didn't want friends. He just used to spin a top and watch it. One day I went there and he was hitting the top with a bat."

Later, he would beg other boys to pitch Coca-Cola caps to him, remembers his father, a retired shipyard worker who once played semi-pro ball in the Mobile area.

"One time when I was nine or ten," Hank says, "I was sitting on the back stoop when an airplane flew overhead. I told my father I would like to be a pilot and he said 'Forget it, there are no black pilots.' And then I said I wanted to be a ballplayer and he said 'Forget about that because there are no black ballplayers.'"

By the time Hank Aaron was 12, there was hope for the black kid who dreamed of playing major league baseball. Jackie Robinson had signed with the Brooklyn Dodgers on Aug. 29, 1945, and been assigned to play for the Montreal Royals, the top Dodger farm club. By 1947, Jackie Robinson was in the National League and Henry Aaron was in Central High School.

Since his school had no baseball team, Hank played

Hank Aaron's parents, Herbert and Estella, cheer his 713th career homer.

softball whenever he could. By his junior year, his hitting and fielding were good enough to win him a job on the semi-pro Mobile Black Bears. He was 16 and a shortstop then. "Some of those players were twenty-one, and maybe older," his mother says proudly. "Some of them even had families."

While he was with the semi-pro team, Hank kept one eye on Jackie Robinson's progress with the Dodgers.

"I can remember cutting a class in high school to hear Jackie Robinson speak at the baseball park in Mobile," says Aaron. "I was supposed to be in shop at the time, but he was going to speak at 2:30 in the afternoon. He talked about baseball and what the future held for black players in the major leagues. That gave me a little hope at that time. I went back and told my father and he said, 'If this is what you want to do, fine, be a baseball player.' He was a very sports-minded man himself and he helped me."

Aaron idolized Robinson the same way white youths idolized Babe Ruth or, in Robinson's time, Ted

Williams. "I had an awful lot of respect for Jackie Robinson," Aaron says today. "The things he went through and the abuse he took getting into the big leagues paved the way for myself and other black players. He was just a great man. I had heard the name Babe Ruth but didn't really know what it meant. I didn't know if he had 714 home runs or if he had 800 home runs. It really didn't matter to me because at that time I had no place to go. There really wasn't any place for blacks in professional ball, so his name didn't haunt me or bother me at all."

Aaron completed his high school education at Mobile's Josephine Allen Institute which, like Central, had no baseball team, but Hank was set with the Black Bears. On the final Sunday of his first season in 1951, the semi-pro club played the barnstorming Indianapolis Clowns of the old Negro American League. For Henry Aaron, it was a fateful meeting.

Earlier that summer, Hank had gone to a Brooklyn Dodger tryout camp in Mobile but was sent away by a scout who said he was too small for the big leagues. Hank never had the chance to take the field. Disappointed but not crushed,

young Hank Aaron continued his all-around fine play for the Mobile Black Bears and enjoyed the water sports around Mobile Bay. He swam and fished in the bay, practices he continues to this day. Then came the game with the Clowns.

Impressed by Aaron's play, scout Ed Scott offered him a contract for $200 per month. Should he turn pro at 17? Hank discussed the question with his parents.

"He was so young, I worried about him," recalls Mrs. Aaron, who eventually agreed to let her son find out if he could make the grade as a professional player. "That's all he wanted to do was play ball, so I let him go."

Herbert Aaron Sr. didn't like the idea, according to his now-famous son. "My father wanted me to go to college," says the Atlanta outfielder. "Sometimes I wonder what my life might have been like if I couldn't play ball."

Finally, Mrs. Aaron won out. She took him to the Mobile bus station and gave him two sandwiches in a brown paper bag plus all the money she had—two dollars. He also had a brown tattered suitcase with him as he began his march into sports history.

Hank took his cross-handed batting stance to

Success of Jackie Robinson (R), here with Clyde Sukeforth, inspired Aaron as youngster.

Indianapolis for the 1952 season, and started out with hits in his first two times at bat. Before long, his league-leading .467 average had attracted the attention of several major league scouts, including Dewey Griggs, the man who finally got his signature on a Braves' contract.

One of the first to approach the 18-year-old shortstop was a man from the Yankees. "I don't remember his name," Aaron says of the New York scout. "He gave me some vague promises. He never offered any money. I think they really didn't want a black player."

A Giants' scout came right to the point with Hank. If he would sign with that club, the scout said, he would get $150 a month—less than he was making with the Clowns—and be assigned to the Class A Sioux Falls team. The Braves offered $350 a month and assignment to Class C Eau Claire, Wisconsin.

While Aaron debated the wisdom of signing with the Boston Braves or New York Giants, the wheels were turning in the front offices of the Braves and the Clowns. Indianapolis owner Syd Pollock was willing to part with Aaron, and planned to sell him to the highest bidder.

According to Braves' traveling secretary Don Davidson, the Boston Braves landed Aaron just 10 minutes before he would have fallen into the hands of the talent-hungry New York Giants. Davidson said the Braves had made a time agreement with the Clowns to purchase Henry's contract but the Giants and other teams continued to pursue the 18-year-old Aaron, who even at that early stage exhibited immense potential.

In his book Caught Short, Davidson describes what happened. "John Quinn, general manager of the Braves, sent scout Dewey Griggs to make a final decision on Aaron. Griggs took one look at Henry and recommended that the Braves pay the $10,000 for his contract. That was considerably more money back in those days than now, and when Quinn asked Dewey if he would pay $10,000 of his own money, the answer was a definite yes. Quinn asked Farm Director John Mullen if he had sent the telegram honoring the time agreement. Mullen turned pale; he had indeed forgotten. If he had waited 10 more minutes to send the telegram, the Giants would have signed Aaron."

The result, obviously, would have been Aaron and Willie Mays in the same outfield. The National League might have folded by this time.

The deal between the Braves and Clowns gave young Henry Aaron an immediate taste of the travel he would encounter when he finally got to the majors; he made his first plane trip from Charlotte, N.C., where the Clowns were playing, to Eau Claire, where he would join his new team.

Though he had abandoned his cross-handed style at the suggestion of Griggs, Aaron remained a great natural hitter. He was an immediate hit at Eau Claire, where he batted .336 in 87 games. But he weighed only 160 pounds at the time—20 below the weight he carried when he reported to the big league spring training camp two years later—and hit just nine homers in 345 times at bat. He had 25 stolen bases.

Hank reported to the

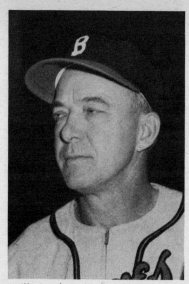
Billy Southworth, then a scout, was impressed by Aaron's play at Eau Claire.

Northern League club after the signing of the contract June 14 and, on July 1, scout Billy Southworth, sent to examine the new Braves' prospect, sent back the following report:

"Aaron has all the qualifications of a major league shortstop. He runs better than average so I would have to call him fast but not very fast. On the latest official Northern League batting averages, he is hitting .345. He is a line drive hitter although he has hit a couple of balls out of the park for home runs. He has good hands, also quick hands, gets ball away fast and accurately. He gets good jump on ball and can range far to right or left. I saw him go deep in the hole to his right and field a slow-hit ball, he came up throwing and virtually shot this man out going to first. This was a big league play in my book because I did not think he had a chance to retire the man at first. He has strong arm.

"Aaron started two double-plays and completed one from the pivot position in his first game. He accepted six chances without an error.

"Aaron throws a lot like Maranville—not overhand but more sidearm. His arm is strong and he does not have to straighten up to throw.

"Aaron told me that he had turned 18 years of age last February; consequently I like his chances of becoming a major league player far more than I do Gene Baker, shortstop of Los Angeles, or James Pendleton of Montreal, first because of the differences in ages; then too I think he has better hands than either Baker or Pendleton. He has proven his ability in the short time he has been here.

"Baker and Pendleton are faster men but this boy will outplay them in all departments of the game when he has had more experience.

"Second Game—On Aaron's first trip to plate, he hit long home run over left-centerfield fence. He collected three hits for the evening and three RBIs. He had four chances with one error. Oh, yes, he also had one stolen base.

"For a baby-faced kid of 18, his playing ability is outstanding.

"I will see the remaining games tonight but will send in this report now, cause regardless of what happens tonight, it will not change my mind in the least about this boy's ability.

"Please don't get the impression from what I have said above that Aaron isn't a good runner 'cause he is **fast** and his running will continue to improve for the next couple of years."

Eau Claire was a good place for a young black player to break in because it was a northern town without any of the shackles of segregation which Aaron later found in the south. Young Henry liked the town, although at one point he got homesick and called his parents to say he was quitting.

Henry spoke to his parents and his younger brother James. Their advice was to stay put. "This is what you always wanted," they told him. "Now don't quit. You stay right there and play ball."

Henry listened, partly because he enjoyed playing in Eau Claire. "It was a beautiful town," he recalls. "There were three other blacks on the team and I had no problem at all. I had many friends at Eau Claire and a lot of them were white."

Life at Eau Claire was the opposite of life at Jacksonville, Fla., where Aaron found himself for the 1953 season. He had earned a promotion to the Class A Sally League, but he had not realized he and another future big leaguer—Felix Mantilla—would be the first blacks in that league, along with another man who never made the big time.

"Jacksonville was the same ballpark that they had barred Jackie Robinson from playing in," Aaron remembers. "They closed the gates on him. You wouldn't believe some of the things we went through. They would call you "jigaboo" and "burrhead" and "nigger."

"Finally, we got together and decided the only way we could defeat this thing was to go out there and play baseball—to do the best we could. All that stuff made me more determined to make people realize I was going to be a major league player and that the only thing I was interested in was playing major league ball. Those things didn't bother me at the time although later on they did bother me."

Aaron's father remembers traveling to Montgomery, Ala., to see Jacksonville play. "When Henry came up, I heard the fans yell 'Hit that nigger. Hit that nigger.' Henry hit the ball up against the clock. The next time he came up, they said 'Walk him, walk him.'"

It was at Jacksonville that Hank met the late Ben Geraghty, whom he still labels the best manager he has ever played for. It's quite a tribute, considering Aaron has played under Charlie Grimm, Fred Haney, Charlie Dressen, Birdie Tebbetts, Bobby Bragan, Billy Hitchcock, Luman Harris, and Eddie Mathews.

It was Geraghty who taught Aaron never to make the same mistake twice. The lesson was learned the hard way—through practical application. There was the day Aaron stole second three times—and was picked off when the second baseman pulled the hidden-ball trick every time. And there were other games for Henry to learn the do's and don'ts of baseball.

In all, Hank hit .362, slammed 22 homers, stole 13 bases, and batted in 125 runs while appearing in 137 games, mostly as a second baseman. He led the league in batting, RBIs, and—still mastering the art of second base play after breaking into pro ball at short—in errors. Still, he was the league's MVP at age 19.

Also in 1953, which, by the way, was the parent club's first year in Milwaukee, Henry Aaron tied the knot with Barbara Lucas, an 18-year-old college coed he met one day near the Jacksonville ballpark.

By the time he was ready for spring training in 1954, Henry Louis Aaron was a father. In addition, he was an outfielder. The Braves, realizing that they were strong in the infield and that Aaron's imposing hitting talents were too great for him to run the risk of injury in the infield, had sent him off to a winter league after the 1953 season to learn the rudiments of outfield play. With his good running speed, excellent baseball instinct, and fine arm, Hank seemed like the ideal outfield candidate. And he was, as he later proved when he won four Gold Glove awards for fielding excellence in the outfield.

Still, Hank was not supposed to make the majors until 1955. He was ticketed for the top Braves' farm at Toledo when he reported to the Bradenton, Fla., camp. He wasn't on the 40-man roster and few of the Milwaukee veterans had heard of him.

"He was just another kid in camp," recalls Eddie Mathews, then the defending NL home run king. "He didn't have that much of a reputation. The Braves always had a lot of good prospects. Nobody paid any attention to him."

Billy Bruton, the fancy centerfielder, recalls his first impression of Aaron. "When he first came up, I used to hold my breath when a fly ball was hit to him," says Bruton. "Then I realized that he always ambled after a ball like that. But he always got to it. After awhile, I stopped worrying."

Shortstop Johnny Logan, a fiery competitor, says of Aaron, "He was all eyes. He was very quiet."

It was at that 1954 spring training camp that Hank Aaron and Eddie Mathews met for the first time. Though the two would go on to become the most prolific home-run hitting teammates in the game's history, no one in camp ever dreamed of matching Mathews, the game's top home run star,

with Aaron, a skinny rookie from a Class A club.

But Aaron was very aware of the big third baseman. "It was natural for me to be very conscious of Eddie, maybe even a little awed by him," he says. "After all, he was a big star, the home run champion of the National League, and I was only a rookie. The chances are that I didn't even introduce myself to him, but just looked at him in the clubhouse and on the field."

Who could have guessed that the team of Mathews and Aaron would go on to hit 963 home runs as teammates, a total never reached by Ruth and Gehrig, Mantle and Maris, Snider and Hodges, or Mays and Mc-Covey? Even Aaron wouldn't have predicted it.

"When I broke in," he says, "I wasn't even a power-hitter. I weighed 160 pounds and hit a total of nine home runs at Eau Claire. It wasn't much to get excited over."

The 20-year-old rookie pretty much escaped notice as he went through the routine of spring training with the major leaguers. Yet he and the other blacks on the team had to cope with the segregation of the Deep South.

"That first spring with the Milwaukee Braves in Bradenton, the white players

Eddie Mathews (L) and Bill Bruton were Braves' stars when Hank joined team.

were staying in one hotel and we were staying on the other side of the railroad tracks," recalls Henry, with a trace of bitterness. "When we would go on trips, leaving for Bradenton to go to Vero Beach to play the Dodgers, we would all take the bus and stop about halfway there for lunch. Either we had to wait for some of the white players to bring us a sandwich on the bus or we would have to find a cab and go across the railroad track to find a sandwich. It was unfair for the simple reason that even though we had to go to the other side of town, they expected us to be back at a certain time to catch the bus. Things like this were tough for us. Everything was separate. You had to live separate, eat separate, and travel practically separate."

For Bruton, who had established himself as a regular the year before, the racial divisions of the six-week training camp could be tolerated. After all, he knew he would be going north with the big league club.

For Aaron, a rookie

Aaron's first big league homer came off Vic Raschi on April 23, 1954.

destined to return to the minors, the treatment accorded the blacks touched a raw nerve. But he never complained out loud.

"Henry never spoke about it; he never made any complaints," said his father. "I believe if you start to worry about complaints, it's going to take a lot from you."

Aaron saved his strength and was ready when opportunity knocked. It happened on March 13, 1954, when Bobby Thomson broke his ankle sliding into third during an exhibition game.

Thomson, author of the pennant-winning "shot heard 'round the world" for the 1951 New York Giants, had just been acquired by the Braves to play left field.

Thomson, whose injury opened the door wide for Henry Aaron, recalls his impressions of the 20-year-old rookie who took his job. "Magic is the only way to describe it," he says. "I mean you just had a feeling—even then—that this guy was something special. He was far removed from the ordinary class of ballplayer, like the rest of us.

"Some of the fellows were a little skeptical, really, when in 1954 the Braves' front office told us this young kid, Henry Aaron, would be in spring training with us. Everybody had said he would bound to be a great one, but nobody gave him much thought. He'd hit well in the minors, sure, but we figured he'd be like so many other rookies before him—come to camp with a reputation, really see the curveball for the first time, and bomb out."

Thomson's injury upset Aaron. "I just remember feeling bad for Bobby," says the man who became his successor in the Milwaukee outfield. "It didn't occur to me at the time that it would be me who would replace him. I thought it would be Jim Pendleton, who'd had a good season the year before. A lot of fellows had had good seasons in Triple-A too and I'd played only two years."

Actually, the choice for manager Charlie Grimm narrowed down to Pendleton or Aaron. Both had done well in winter ball, but Aaron was younger and had had a fine spring. Pendleton, on the other hand, had been involved in a salary dispute.

The next day, March 14, 1954, Henry Louis Aaron made his first start in an exhibition game. The Braves were playing the Boston Red Sox, whose most famous player was Ted Williams, then the world's ranking authority on hitting.

During batting practice that day, Williams was sitting in the Boston dugout, talking to his usual mob of sportswriters. Aaron in the batting cage, suddenly made contact with a pitch. The sharp "crrrraccckkk" could be heard all over the ballpark.

Williams turned around and asked, "Who the hell hit that?"

Informed it was "Aaron, the new kid from Jacksonville," Ted made a prophetic statement: "He sounds like a hell of a hitter."

Aaron made three hits in the game, including a long home run, and sewed up the Braves' leftfield job. When Thomson returned to his leftfield stand in 1955, Hank moved to right, where he starred through the 1970 season, with a two-year interruption in 1961 and 1962, when he filled the Milwaukee centerfield hole created by the trade of Bruton to Detroit. He spent the 1971 and 1972 seasons as a first baseman before realizing that both he and the team are better off with him in the outfield. The passing of time weakened his once-powerful throwing arm, however, and it is ironic that Aaron is now concluding his big league career in leftfield, the same position at which he began it.

The 20-year-old outfielder was a quiet, reserved rookie, but he made a set of secret personal goals when he made the big league team. "When I first joined the Milwaukee Braves, I set a goal then—I would like to play ball 20 years and I would like to be successful at playing," he states.

"I said I would like to accomplish certain things—I set my goal kind of high. I wanted to get 3,000 base-hits, I wasn't thinking in terms of seven hundred home runs, of course, but I was thinking in terms of hitting more than four hundred home runs in my career. I felt if I could achieve these two goals, I could be fairly successful in baseball."

Even though he broke into the majors seven years after Jackie Robinson first came up with the Dodgers, there were still only a few blacks in the big leagues and those who were there had to be good.

"In the first few years, I felt there was pressure on the black ballplayer," Aaron admits today. "At that time there were so few black

Late Rogers Hornsby recognized young Aaron as a potentially great hitter.

ballplayers that in order for you to be on a ballclub, you couldn't be a fringe player. You had to be able to do twice as many things as the white players.

"Some of the white players sitting on the bench were making twice as much money as you were, but you were out there playing every day."

The responsibilities of being a regular meant Aaron had to master all kinds of pitches and all kinds of deliveries. One pitch which gave him trouble in 1954 was the change-up. When he came up that spring, he couldn't hit it.

"Jacksonville was in the

Sally League, a fastball league," Hank says. "In the majors, I had to learn to hit the off-speed stuff. I learned to hit the change-up off Carl Erskine of the Brooklyn Dodgers. I just said to myself that I was going to wait on the pitch and be patient."

Aaron began 1954 wearing No. 5—a typical number for an infielder (current second baseman Dave Johnson wears No. 6)—but soon asked Don Davidson, then publicity director, for a double numeral. Davidson protested, saying, "All the great hitters wore low numbers, like Ruth's 3, Gehrig's 4, DiMaggio's 5, Musial's 6, Mantle's 7, and Williams' 9." But Aaron persisted, perhaps because black stars Willie Mays (24) and Jackie Robinson (42) had been successful wearing double numerals.

"I finally assigned him 44," said Davidson, "and four times in his career, he's hit 44 home runs, so I regret that I did not give him number 70."

Regardless of his number, Henry Aaron was on his way toward baseball immortality when he belted a Vic Raschi pitch for his first home run on April 23, 1954, in the fourth inning at St. Louis. Though no one knew it at the time, the blow represented "1 down, 714 to go."

Raschi remembers the game. "Nobody on our team seemed to know anything about Aaron except Eddie Stanky, the manager," he says, recalling the pre-game rundown on the opposing line-up. "He knew that Henry was potentially a fine player, and he talked about everything except the way he parted his hair. He could run, field, throw, and, of course, hit. He had such great wrists, like Ernie Banks, it was hard to fool him."

Aaron took well to the city of Milwaukee, just as he took well to his new diet of National League pitching. "I've never had anything but good feelings for Milwaukee," he reported. "It's a wonderful town, and the people were very kind to me. I always lived in integrated neighborhoods, without problems.

For Aaron, his main worry was making a mark for himself in the tough National League.

Almost immediately, he was recognized as a "sleepy hitter" at the plate—until he swung the bat, that is. Once, after hitting a long home run off Robin Roberts, then the best righthander in the league, Aaron returned to the Milwaukee dugout and amazed a teammate when he

Aaron and Eddie Mathews became a great homer-hitting tandem for the Braves.

asked, "Is that really Roberts out there?"

It wasn't long before the smooth Aaron swing had attracted attention all around the league. Even Hall of Famer Rogers Hornsby, who served as batting coach for the Cubs in the 1950s, talked about young Aaron.

"Henry is a wrist hitter, all good hitters are," said the former slugging second baseman, whose .424 one-season batting record still stands. "He has the kind of wrists and whip swing that enable him to wait until the last split second and to get a piece of the ball even on pitches that have fooled him. Breaking the wrists means follow through for power. Players who stand flat-footed and swing with their arms are golfers, not hitters.

"Somebody has said that Aaron has great hips. Hips?

Hell, you don't hit a baseball with your rear end. What Aaron has is a smooth pivot that gives him power. He has made use of what the good Lord gave him—the eyes, arms, legs, and coordination of a natural hitter.

"If he pays attention to the strike zone, it doesn't make any difference who the pitcher is, what arm he throws with, or what the pitch is. If Aaron makes them put the ball in there, he can hit it.

"Aaron can become an even better hitter than he is—maybe even a .400 hitter—with enough desire," continued Hornsby. "In addition to all the natural ability in the world, it takes heart, call it guts, and desire. I became a hitter because I wanted to bad enough."

The late Hornsby, rated by most experts as the best

second baseman who ever played the game, concluded his summation of the young Henry as follows: "He hits with power to all fields and that's the test of a hitter— hitting the ball where it's pitched. That takes timing."

Johnny Logan recalls, "Hank was a line-drive hitter, but he fell in with Eddie Mathews and Joe Adcock and said, 'Hmmmm, I can hit with these guys.' Then it seemed that every time Eddie hit a homer, Hank would follow with a homer in that game or the next one."

It wasn't until the 1955 season, when Hank more than doubled his rookie home run output of 13, that he was recognized as a long-ball threat. "It was probably in mid-season of 1955 before I realized Aaron was a home run hitter," says Mathews. "His power was to right and right-center. That meant he would hit more homers as he grew older and learned to pull the ball."

Aaron himself admitted, "I didn't begin to think of myself as a home run hitter until I was around a few years. When I was a rookie in 1954, we had Eddie Mathews and Joe Adcock and I considered myself a guy who got on base. But when I got older and stronger, I also got more selective with the pitches I hit, and that turned me into a home run hitter. Then it was my responsibility."

As a rookie in 1954, Henry Aaron hit .280 in a season curtailed by a broken ankle suffered Sept. 5. It was the only major injury of his long career—the only one which kept him out of the line-up for a prolonged length of time. He finished second to Wally Moon of the St. Louis Cardinals in the balloting for NL Rookie of the Year, but won the Most Valuable Brave citation from the Milwaukee chapter of the Baseball Writers Association of America. It was the first of many such awards for Henry Aaron, who in 1969 was voted by the fans as the Greatest Brave Ever, ahead of Eddie Mathews and Warren Spahn.

It is hard to imagine that the mighty ending of the Hank Aaron story which America will witness in 1974 all began 21 springs ago in the segregated training camp town of Bradenton, Florida. And it is even harder to imagine that the man about to inherit the mantle of home run supremacy is the same individual who was a skinny, scared, 20-year-old kid not even on the big league roster that spring.

Henry Louis Aaron has come a long way. ●

THE HENRY AARON I KNOW

■ Hank Aaron's status as the brightest star of his era and one of the all-time greats is reflected in the tributes paid to him by his colleagues— opponents as well as teammates.

"What do I think of Hank Aaron? That's easy. Aaron is the greatest player in the history of baseball," says Ralph Garr, who took over Aaron's old rightfield spot with the Braves in 1973.

Another teammate, Darrell Evans, observes, "He's the No. 1 story in baseball. The guy is finally getting what's due him. I'm excited over it too. I'll be the first to congratulate him when he gets 715. Hank has shown me a lot about the strike zone and waiting for my pitch. (Evans had 41 homers and 104 runs batted to earn the starting third base position on the Associated Press' all-major league team). Now I go up to the plate feeling like I can hit a home run every time."

Second baseman Dave Johnson, who finished second in the 1973 AP all-star balloting to Minnesota's Rod Carew, joined the Braves for the 1973 season and got to see Aaron enjoy one of his best seasons. Of Aaron, Johnson says: "Henry's going to get his homers anywhere. He doesn't just scrape the back of the wall when he hits them."

Dusty Baker, the 24-year-old outfielder who many rank as Aaron's heir apparent with the team, shrugs off the inevitable comparison with the team's top star. "I can never be a Hank Aaron," he says. "I don't think there will ever be another Hank Aaron. I just want to be the first Dusty Baker. It would be so beautiful if we could win a pennant and get into the World Series before Hank retires. I think that would be a tremendous tribute to the man. You know, he's contributed so much to the club and the places we've come in the last two or three years haven't been what he deserved."

Former teammate Felipe Alou, who has also played for

Hank Aaron follows through smoothly after belting No. 699 at Atlanta Stadium.

the Giants and Expos in the National League, says: "I never realized how good Henry was out there until I played alongside him. You can't tell watching from the other side. He makes it look so easy."

Another former teammate, Clete Boyer, adds: "He knows more about baseball than any man I have ever met."

Baltimore catcher-first baseman Earl Williams is one of many young players who were impressed when they first met Aaron—not only by his all-around skills of the field but also by his quiet leadership in the clubhouse.

"I first met Hank in 1966," recalls Williams, who was traded by the Braves after the 1972 season, "and he impressed me immediately as a man with a lot of class. He carries himself well and he is a quiet, soft-spoken guy."

Williams was a rookie with a tough assignment for the 1971 Braves. He was a first and third baseman who had to make a mid-season conversion to catcher, the toughest defensive position, without prior experience. It was a difficult psychological as well as physical adjustment, but Aaron helped the rookie make the move successfully.

"As the year went on, he more or less took me under his wing, but it wasn't an active thing," says Williams, who went on to sock 33 homers and win the NL's Rookie-of-the-Year Award that season.

"He didn't just take me from the beginning of the year. It was a thing that grew gradually. It wasn't pushed on either part. I could come to him with questions and problems and he would help me," Williams says.

Eddie Mathews, current Braves' manager and a former star third baseman, team captain and coach with the team, has followed Aaron's career at close range for all but four of The Hammer's 20 major league seasons through 1973.

"I've known Hank since 1954 as a teammate, coach, manager, and friend, and respect him as a great baseball player and a splendid person," says Mathews of his meal-ticket.

"Hank makes things look so easy that people sometimes wonder if he is extending himself. It was that way back in 1954 when he was a rookie and it's that way today when he is a veteran of more than 3,000 major league games. I can assure you he always gives 100 per cent.

"Hank has shown me a lot about the strike zone," says Darrell Evans.

Mathews also has high praise for Aaron because of the super-star's cooperative attitude and easy-going disposition.

"We've always been able to sit down and get close to each other by talking things over," the Braves' manager says.

"From a manager's standpoint, he is a great guy to have on the club. You can always work out something with him—whether it directly affects him or whether you would like him to give some advice to a young player—which is why we don't have any trouble finding a formula for his playing schedule."

Mathews, sticking to the schedule arrangement worked out with Aaron prior to the 1973 campaign, rested his slugger just enough so that he retained his strength through the whole season. If anything, Henry got stronger as the season progressed, hitting .398 after the July 24 All-Star Game.

"When I think of Hank's career," observes Mathews, "one word comes to mind: consistency. The test of a major league star is the ability to sustain excellence over a long period of time."

Aaron certainly has done that, as a check of the record reveals. White Sox personnel director Roland Hemond, an

"Hank is essentially a competitor and, like all good athletes, he regards winning as more important than accumulating statistics," continues the manager, in an obvious reference to Aaron's pursuit of Babe Ruth's home run record.

"That 714 statistic is the biggest one in the record book, of course, but even so I think Hank's greatest desire is to play in another World Series. It seems like only yesterday that he helped make it come true in Milwaukee, so perhaps it will only be tomorrow when he helps to make it come true in Atlanta."

admirer from the American League, is one of many baseball people who are amazed by Aaron's solid performance, year in, year out, particularly in view of his advancing age. Hank turned 40 before the first ball was thrown in the 1974 spring training camps.

"If there is anything I notice different about Hank Aaron," says Hemond, "it's that he seems to be getting better as he gets older."

New York Mets' pitcher Tom Seaver, who arrived in the majors in 1967, says Aaron is still an inspiration to him—though the two are deadly enemies when the Braves play the Mets.

"When I was a youngster," recalls Seaver, "Henry Aaron was the supreme type of ballplayer that I wanted to be. He was a dedicated man with super ability. My impressions of him never changed. The thoughts and ideas I had of Henry Aaron as a youngster, he's lived up to in the big leagues. One of my big thrills is to be able to pitch against him today."

Another Met, outfielder Cleon Jones, knows Aaron even better than Seaver because he was the batboy for the Mobile Black Bears when Aaron was a teen-aged sensation with that black semi-pro outfit.

"He's a super human being," says Jones of Aaron, "not only on the ballfield but in life in general. As big as he is, he's so modest that he walks into a place and people never knows he's there. But if one person, or two, or 20 ask him for his autograph, he always signs and gives them a smile."

National League pitchers become very much aware of Hank Aaron as soon as they've faced him once or twice.

Seaver says: "Henry was one of my idols. I knew his every mannerism. Soon I realized that I was just standing there watching him, and I had to turn away toward centerfield. The first time up, he hit into a doubleplay. Then he put one in the seats and my love affair with him was over."

Another star righthander, Don Sutton of the Los Angeles Dodgers, recalls his first meeting with Hank during a game. The Hammer had been preceded by his reputation, as he is everywhere he goes, but Sutton retired him easily the first three times up in the 1966 contest. Pop up, ground out, strikeout. "Hank Aaron—big deal," Sutton said to himself.

The fourth time up, the Dodger rightly tried a fastball

"I can never be another Hank Aaron," confesses Braves' young star Dusty Baker.

on the inside corner, the same pitch Aaron had made an out on earlier. A quick snap of the wrists sent the ball on a line over the leftfield fence. "He's so smart," said Sutton, "you can't keep getting him out the same way."

Don Davidson, the diminutive Atlanta front office dynamo, summed up many of the pitchers' feelings when he said, "Hank Aaron is without a doubt the greatest righthanded hitter I've ever seen—ahead of Joe DiMaggio."

Los Angeles columnist Jim Murray, one of the nation's truly outstanding sports-writers, went one step further than Davidson. He wrote, "Grace under pressure is courage. Grace under pressure without effort is genius. Observe Henry Aaron going after a fly ball. That hat doesn't fly off. Wheels aren't coming off. He

Ex-Brave Felipe Alou says Aaron makes everything look so easy out there."

is indeed a great tribute to Aaron. But there's a universal sentiment throughout the game that the Atlanta star deserves it.

"When you go to rating baseball's all-time best players," says Cincinnati pilot Sparky Anderson, "he's gotta be in the top ten."

Cardinal manager Red Schoendienst, who played second base for the championship Braves teams in 1957 and 1958, says, "Good hitters just play. Bad hitters become politicians and try to hang on that way. Henry's just a natural-born hitter."

Hall of Famer Stan Musial, a man Aaron has admired for a long time, adds, "Hank's a different kind of power hitter. He makes contact, doesn't strike out much. When you don't strike out much, you're doing something with the ball, which is important."

Another member of the Hall, Hank Greenberg, states, "Hank Aaron is about the only good hitter left in the major leagues. He's one of the few who can still hit consistently and hit the long ball too."

A writer who has observed Aaron since the Braves came to Atlanta in 1966 is Jesse Outlar, sports editor of the Atlanta Constitution. His poetic description of Aaron cannot be overlooked. He

doesn't look like a man fighting off a swarm of bees. He looks as if he's LOAFING, for crying out loud! But if you get a clock on him you will find he has just broken the 20-yard dash record for rightfielders."

Aaron now is a leftfielder, of course, but his defensive work was dazzling at that position, particularly after the All-Star break in 1973.

When Lou Boudreau entered the baseball Hall of Fame, he said, "I'm really humbled by this because I never considered myself a super-star like Williams, DiMaggio or Aaron."

To be placed in such company by a Hall of Famer

Eddie Mathews (R) says Aaron likes winning more than accumulating statistics.

Baseball great Leo Durocher says Aaron has "class based on quiet competence."

wrote,"Aaron's achievements are sufficient to enlarge any cranium, but success hasn't spoiled Henry. He's also a major leaguer off the diamond. On the field, he is an artist, a Rembrandt with a baseball bat, and it's worth the price of admission to watch Henry Aaron play the game."

The veteran Atlanta outfielder is an inspiration to blacks both in the game and in the baseball audience. "All the black players who play in the major leagues identify with Hank Aaron because he is a tremendous man and he is going for a tremendous record," explains Ernie Banks, hitting instructor and former great slugger of the Chicago Cubs.

"Our people have lived as underdogs, and when he finally does something no one else does it's a sense of real achievement," says Billye Aaron, who married the

Braves' star after the 1973 season ended. "I don't think he's taking anything away from Babe Ruth. It's a matter of any man feeling it can be done. Breaking a record is always a challenge."

Gaile Aaron, Hank's 20-year-old daughter by his first marriage, is a journalism major at Fisk University who described her father in a special newspaper article near the end of the 1973 season.

She wrote: "In my estimation, Hank Aaron is not a two-legged home run machine. He is a mild-mannered, concerned person with human interests, giving great concern for his four children—Hank Jr., Larry, Dorinda, and myself—their education, and their future. During his 20-year career, daddy has received many gifts, trophies and proclamations, but I still feel his most cherished gift is Dorinda, presented to him 11 years ago on his birthday. . . . As I sit in the stands and hear the fans applaud for Mr. Brave, it makes me feel good to know that this is my father they love."

According to the Rev. Michael Sablica, philosophy professor at the Catholic Seminary Foundation in Indianapolis and the man who converted Aaron from Baptist to Catholic when the Braves played in Milwaukee, "Hank is a very unusual human being. He has a naturally good mind and you can't help sensing that his consciousness has evolved to a high level. His mental and physical preparation for a game is remarkable."

That preparation has enabled Aaron to set nearly two-dozen significant records involving performance, endurance and consistent ranking far above most of his contemporaries.

"He has class but it's based on a quiet competence," says Leo Durocher of the Atlanta star, always a thorn in the side of Leo and his pitchers. "He lacks in emotional outbursts, so only the wiser heads accept him for what he is—one of the greatest, and I mean one of the all-time greatest."

His batting style is remembered by Curt Simmons, the lefthander who starred for the Phillies and Cardinals and always gave Aaron fits. "Henry Aaron is the only ballplayer I know," he says, "who goes to sleep at the plate and wakes up only to swing as the pitch comes in."

Another ex-pitcher, Ron Herbel, played with both Aaron and Willie Mays during his career. When he was traded to the Braves, he said, "I've been on a club with Mays and now with Aaron ... two super-stars. And I sure won't miss pitching to Aaron."

Lefthander George Stone, once a member of the Braves, was as awestruck by Aaron as a teammate, and he is now that Hank is an enemy batsman. "That Aaron is just unreal," he says. "He just keeps on going. I see him, but I don't believe what I am seeing."

"Just when you've thrown the ball by him, he's got the bat around so fast that he almost takes the ball out of the catcher's glove," explains Ferguson Jenkins, who at one stretch won 20 games or more for six straight years while working for the Chicago Cubs—even though he had to face Aaron.

Gary Nolan, another righthander who faced Aaron often, states "When that guy hits one, you don't think anything of it. You just get a new ball and go onto the next hitter."

Steve Blass, also a member of the pitching fraternity, comments: "He's very menacing, He's gotta be up there in front of or at least even with every other power-hitter in baseball."

Pitcher Dock Ellis has one rule about pitching Aaron.

"Henry's just a natural-born hitter," maintains ex-teammate Red Schoendienst.

"We gotta keep it down," he said. "That's the only thing we think about."

Though he is proud that a black man will inherit the career home run mantle, Ellis notes, "Blacks would have all the records if we had played. If a record is made, we're going to break them."

Ellis is bitter that blacks were denied the opportunity to play in the majors before 1947, but he emphasizes that there is no racial hostility on the field. "I don't think being black hurts Aaron because any time you're out there in a competitive sport like baseball, it's impossible to do something like that."

Certainly, no one thinks "black man" when Hank Aaron steps to the plate. The thoughts running through the rival pitcher's and rival manager's minds must be "Hank Aaron," or "No. 44," or "The Hammer," or "don't-let-this-guy-beat-you."

Sandy Koufax and Don Drysdale, for example, referred to Aaron as "Bad Henry" because of the pain he inflicted on their normally superb earned run averages.

When Koufax, the great lefthander of the Dodgers, was named Player of the Decade for the 1960s by The Associated Press, he said, "I think it's incredible because there were guys like Mays and Mantle and Henry Aaron who were great players for 10 years . . . I only had four or five good years."

The southpaw remembers facing Aaron on the baseball battlefield. "When Aaron walked up to the plate, he was so relaxed he looked as if he were sleeping," says Koufax. "He looked that way until he swung the bat."

Koufax had a great fastball and a great curve, but Aaron managed seven career homers off him. Former Milwaukee manager Fred Haney knew why. Asked who the best fastball or best curveball hitters were, he said simply, "Aaron happens to be both."

Next to the rival pitcher and catcher, and the Braves' on-deck hitter, the person closest to Aaron—not counting the umpire—is the Atlanta batboy. Kevin Barnes, a Georgia State University journalism student, held the position in 1973.

Barnes says: "He always looks at the pitchers and studies them very closely. Possibly, he'll look at the batter who's up just before him to see if he's doing anything wrong, to see if he can adjust something, and he'll tell him later when he sits down on the bench.

"Aaron is a real nice guy," Barnes continued. "He jokes around a lot with the players and everything and he's always been pretty friendly with me. No complaints that way."

No one has any complaints about Hank Aaron . . . not even his opponents. They admire him from the rival dugouts, and look at his achievements with a kind of awe. A man like this comes into baseball only once in a generation and the game will miss him when he passes into retirement. This man, this Henry Aaron, is the personification of un-surpassed excellence. •

A PRIVATE MAN

■ Until the 1973 season started, Henry Aaron had always been known as a man with remarkable baseball skills and a penchant for living a private life off the field.

Unlike other athletes who kept the press posted on their nocturnal exploits, Aaron always kept to himself. He simply wasn't the flamboyant type either on or off the field. His personality did not recall the legend of the high-living Babe Ruth, the swinging playboy-pitcher Bo Belinsky, or the electric Willie Mays.

Henry Aaron would have preferred to retain the privacy of his personal life in 1973 and to continue it in 1974, but the spotlight of publicity often denied him that right as he made his final drive toward Babe Ruth's home run record. That drive has turned Hank Aaron into an international celebrity.

Eddie Mathews, now the manager of the Braves, recalled that Aaron never announced his personal plans to the newsmen or to his teammates. "In the Milwaukee days, a lot of players would have favorite bars," he says. "They'd meet there and then take off in different directions. The next day in the clubhouse, guys would be telling stories about the women they had or how much they drank. I'd ask Henry what he did. He'd just smile and say 'I was out.'"

Aaron himself admits he likes certain restaurants—among them Mamma Leone's in New York and Leb's in Atlanta—and says his favorite is Smith's, a modest Atlanta establishment which offers what Aaron calls "the best food in town." He craves seafood, especially the fresh gulf fish and shrimp his father regularly brings to Atlanta when he comes up from Mobile, and a waitress at Leb's, a Kosher restaurant, confirms that he always orders the same fish dish.

Asked what he liked about Mamma Leone's, the famous Italian eatery in New York, Aaron declined a specific answer. Instead, he replied,

Basically, Hank Aaron is a private person who shuns the public spotlight.

"It's a good place and you have to eat somewhere, don't you?"

Though Aaron's visits to restaurants and other public places are made somewhat uncomfortable for him because of constant requests for autographs (his face is easily recognizable these days) he enjoys going out and relaxing. "I need to relax and enjoy myself once in awhile like anyone else," he said one day near the end of the 1973 season.

He hardly had time for relaxation in the heat of his chase of Ruth's record, but he made time after the season ended. He took a post-season fishing trip in Mobile Bay not long after the Braves closed their campaign with a 6-3 loss to Houston on Sept. 30. "I've always liked to fish," he says. "Everybody around Mobile does. The fishing is so good, you'd be crazy not to. I go out almost every day when I'm in Mobile and catch mostly sailfish in the bay."

The slugger also spent the 1973-74 off-season swimming—it helps him keep his trim figure—and playing handball, activities he undertakes between seasons every year. In addition, he made numerous television appearances, including guest shots with Flip Wilson and

Aaron and TV commentator Billye Williams were married after 1973 season.

Merv Griffin, and was the subject of an hour-long NBC special, "The Long Winter of Henry Aaron." The special underlined the significance of the record Aaron approaches; it was produced by the network's news department rather than sports department.

Aaron also got married—for the second time—two months after the 1973 season ended. His wife, the former Billye Williams, is an Atlanta TV commentator who first met Henry two years earlier, when she was assigned to interview several Braves. "I was only dimly aware of his existence or of the Braves at that time," she recalls with a laugh. "I had never seen the team play."

124

Now Billye is as much a regular in the Atlanta Stadium stands as her husband is on the field. "You should see the way we jump up and down when Hank gets a homer," says Carla Koplin, a secretary assigned to handle the slugger's mail and other mattters. "She's very cool otherwise, but then she shouts and yells as we hug each other."

Aaron is a very dedicated family man who is close to his parents, his brothers and sisters, and his four children by his first marriage. He was raised in the tight-knit atmosphere created by the economic realities of the Great Depression. Everyone had to stick together.

"My father made $115 a week when he worked, but the only thing was he would work a week and be laid off two," Aaron remembers. "He only worked when the docks had work. We just did without meat when my father got laid off. We had a garden out back of the house where we'd grow beans and tomatoes and a little okra. I never remember being real hungry."

Herbert and Estella Aaron had a total of seven mouths to feed, not counting their own. They would have had an eighth but they lost a son to pneumonia at an early age.

Today, Aaron's three sisters—Sarah, Gloria and Alfredia—are housewives who still live in Mobile. Tommie, who spent some time as Hank's teammate with the Braves, is the successful manager of the Double-A Savannah Braves in the Southern League. The other Aaron brothers are James, who helped talk Aaron out of early retirement when 18-year-old Henry got homesick at Eau Claire, and Herbert, who might have preceded Hank into professional baseball if Army service hadn't interfered.

The relationship between Hank and Tommie has special significance because the two were teammates for a number of seasons in the majors. Even so, Hank strongly believes his younger brother did not get a fair chance in the Braves' organization.

"Tommie never had the opportunity to prove what he could do with this club," says Henry, "because the Braves never played him enough. I know he could have been a very good ballplayer if he'd signed up with somebody other than the Braves."

The 6-1, 200-pounder was signed for the Braves by scout Hugh Wise on May 28, 1958, when Henry was already in his fifth full season. After several productive seasons in the minors, Tommie finally made it to Milwaukee in 1962. He was a classic fielder at first base, his best position defensively, but he could also play second, third, and the outfield. He seemed like the ideal handyman; he could hit, hit with power, and play almost anywhere.

But the jump from Austin of the Texas League to Milwaukee of the National was a bit too much for Tommie, who got off to a slow start. However, he rebounded for a strong second half and had final figures of .231 with eight home runs in 141 games. It wasn't enough for the Braves, although it proved to be the best of his four full seasons in the majors. Tommie spent a number of years shuttling between the Braves and the minors, then finally came back to the majors as an Atlanta Brave in 1968, 1969 and 1970. He hit .250 in 1969 as the Braves won the NL West, but he batted just 60 times.

"It just seems they never gave me a chance," claims Tommie, who began the 1973 season as a player-coach with Savannah before taking over as manager on June 15. "But hell, not everyone can be Hank Aaron. That guy's unique in the world."

Though the Aaron name apparently hurt Tommie—of whom everyone expected a Herculean performance—it did help get him in the record books. He and Henry combined for 726 home runs, more than any brother combination had ever produced. Even the three DiMaggios and the three Alous could not match that production. Of course, of the 726, Hank has 713 and Tommie 13.

Despite the disappointments (to both brothers) of Tommie's career with the Braves, there are now things to look forward to. In 1973, Tommie became the highest-ranking black manager in baseball and Henry reached within striking distance of Babe Ruth's record. Both men had attained lofty objectives that had not been achieved before. And each cheered the other's accomplishments.

"The day he breaks the record," says Tommie of Hank, "I think I'll feel just as happy as he will—probably happier. Look, he's my brother. I love him. I keep watching the papers every day, and anytime he hits a home run, I feel great."

Tommie, like Henry, has been pestered with one main question from reporters. While Hank talks about Babe

Ruth, Tommie talks about Hank.

"You couldn't compare Hank and me," he said last season before a game in Savannah. "We're two different style ballplayers. He is the complete ballplayer; he can do just about anything. I had to scuffle to do it."

Older brother Henry, learning Tommie got the Savannah job over several other qualified applicants, said, "I'm really pleased for him. Tommie has a good baseball mind and I think he'll be a good manager. I just hope the people won't get the idea that the Braves gave him the job because of me. That's not the way it was. Tommie earned it on his own and he'll hold it on his own."

Tommie Aaron, Hank's brother, is now a manager in the Braves' farm system.

The Aaron parents have cases of trophies and many scrapbooks thick with yellowed clippings about their sons' exploits. Most are about Henry, of course. "I try to tell my wife she can't save every scrap of paper about him," laughs Herbert Aaron, "but she won't listen."

Mrs. Aaron admits, "I don't have space left on the wall to match the size of your hand." The wall she referred to is in a den added to the house several years ago.

The Aarons witnessed a number of their famous son's home runs in 1973 and will be back in Atlanta Stadium many times in 1974, the last season anyone will see Henry Aaron do his thing on a baseball diamond. After that, he'll swing only in movie clips or old-timers games.

One reason Aaron plans to retire is the constant travel. The big reason, though, is his family. Henry Aaron knows his children are almost adults and he wants them to know what it's like to have a full-time father.

"I want to see my kids grow up," Hank told a writer asking why he was so set on retirement after the 1974 season.

The oldest of his four children is Gaile, 20, a journalism major at Fisk University in Nashville, Tenn.

who could someday be interviewing her father if he lands the baseball executive position he seeks after retiring as a player.

"My daughter and I are very close," says Aaron, whose other children include Hank Jr., 17; Larry, 16; and Dorinda, 12. "She's in college at Fisk University and we talk about twice a week. She calls me up and congratulates me every time I hit a home run. Sometimes it gets a little expensive. . .

"I'm quite close with all my kids," continues the mild-mannered star. "The oldest boy wants to play football. He's pretty close to his coach and his teammates. I want him to get into things that he wants to get into—rather than doing things simply because he's Hank Aaron's son. Sometimes I think I should have named him anything but Hank Jr. It might be too much of a burden on him and that would be very unfair."

Aaron's three youngest children go to private schools in Atlanta and probably will continue on to college like their older sister. "My father wanted me to go to college," Hank remembers. "Sometimes I wonder what my life might have been like if I couldn't play ball."

Gaile Aaron pleased her famous father with a front-page bylined story in the Nashville Tennesseean in 1973, and later made headlines with a special syndicated story about her father and the pressures involved in the Babe Ruth race. Part of that story explained the family's feelings about Aaron's accomplishments. It read:

"Hank Aaron is under tremendous pressure, but even we as a family can't really detect it. I guess it's because of his keen sense of humor. There is a different Hank Aaron than the one the public knnows. In my opinion, he is the greatest in baseball, but he could most definitely use some pointers on telling jokes—well maybe on the punch lines!

"Nevertheless, he manages to cheer you up regardless of the situation. On the other hand, he is a man of his word. Soft-spoken he may be, but if the point is to be gotten across, you get it loud and clear. I can never remember him spanking a great deal. He has this approach he uses, with a soft tone of voice that will tear your heart out without even touching you.

"As an ending note, I would like to express the importance of Babe Ruth's record not only to my father and his family, but also to black people and the youngsters of America. It is not everyday that something like this takes place in a person's lifetime.

"This achievement is being accomplished by a black man. This points out to the youth of America that if effort is put forth and patience is insured, accomplishments are possible, keeping in mind that time is an important factor; after all this is the first time in 40 years this record has been challenged."

Billye Aaron agrees with Gaile that Henry has a keen sense of humor. "He's a fantastic person and he's a fun guy although he doesn't come on to be because he appears to be very serious all the time," she observes. "And yet he has a way of breaking out of that shell."

Aaron's sense of humor was readily apparent to the troupe of journalists who tailed him in 1973. When he's with his teammates in the clubhouse or joking with newsmen after a game, he smiles easily and often. Like many athletes, he feels a loose, relaxed frame of mind often helps build a winning ballclub, with every man pulling for everyone else.

In the 1958 World Series, Henry Aaron was loose. Once he came to bat with the label facing toward the pitcher—a no-no in any batting book. Yankee catcher Yogi Berra noticed and asked Hank about it. Aaron's reaction? "I didn't come up here to read," he said. Berra, now the manager of the New York Mets, is still trying to figure him out.

Halfway through the 1973 season, Aaron again used a baseball situation as the basis for a witty remark. Cincinnati catcher Johnny Bench, long an admirer of Henry, sent the Atlanta slugger a picture and asked him to autograph it. The picture showed Aaron sliding safely across home plate in front of Bench, who received a late throw.

The Hammer inscribed it, "To John—try to stay the hell out of my way!"

Not long after Hank signed the photo for Bench, a writer asked him if he considered himself lucky to have spent his entire career with the Braves. The slugger responded, "No, they're lucky."

Aaron also announced he would have a special way to run around the bases following his 714th and 715th home runs. He said he would do it a different way each time.

Someone asked if he would run backwards, as Jimmy Piersall did when he ham-

Cincinnati slugger Johnny Bench has been a long-time admirer of Hank Aaron.

mered his 100th homer for the New York Mets nearly a decade earlier. "I may just **crawl** around the bases," he said, implying it would be a welcome relief to get on the other side of the two huge milestones.

A notorious guess hitter, Aaron also says: "I never guess on two things. One is a third strike. When I have only one pitch coming in, it has to be over the plate and if it is, it doesn't matter what it is.

"The other is that I'll hit— next season or any other. I just keep swinging."

Prior to the last game of the 1973 season, Henry was asked if he would have any trouble sleeping, since that last game could turn into a historic contest if he hit one homer—to tie Babe Ruth—or two to break the all-time record.

Aaron, once accused by Curt Simmons of catching up on his sleep between pitches, had a quick answer. "I never have any trouble sleeping," he said.

Hank's humor is generally dry and to the point. When he signed with WMA Sports, Inc., a subsidiary of the famed William Morris Agency, a talent management firm, it was announced that the baseball star would do commercials and make endorsements. Newsmen at the press conference in the Atlanta Internationale Hotel asked Hank if he'd be doing any singing or dancing in the spots he would do.

"I can't sing and I can't dance," he confessed, "so there's no use in making a fool of myself. I don't think that's what we're talking about. At least, I **hope** not!"

There was the day not too many seasons ago when

Hank was talking with a reporter about Cesar Cedeno, the brilliant young outfielder of the Houston Astros. The writer asked Aaron who was the last player to come into the National League with the potential that could match Cedeno's. Aaron said, "Me."

The home run race also got a needle from The Hammer. "I was on the Atlanta Stadium Authority for four years," he said. "The one recommendation I made was to bring in the fences five feet. Now that I'm not on the Authority, they're moving the fence back five feet, but only in rightfield. You know, I haven't hit a ball to rightfield in six years. They're leaving the leftfield fence alone."

The super-star is also thinking about the record and beyond. "How can I forget it?" he asks. "I'd like to play until I can't anymore. Then I'll take a full year off and get to think like the average man. I won't have to jump out of the way of curve balls in my sleep."

For now, Aaron is still a devastating hitter who can handle a curve ball, fastball or screwball with a smooth skill that gives the impression of indifference. "I've never been a dump hitter," he says. "I have confidence in what I'm doing. I'm either

going to scare the pitcher to death by not hitting the ball or hit it."

He once said about the war between the batter and the pitcher: "The percentage in weapons is in my favor and I let the fellow with the ball do the fretting."

Someone asked him what he looks for when he's at bat and Aaron responded, "The baseball."

Once, when told he had been fined $25 for a minor infraction by Ford Frick, then the Commissioner of Baseball, Aaron asked, "Who's he?"

Today, of course, Aaron knows that Bowie Kuhn is Commissioner. He sat with Kuhn at the opening of the 1973 World Series and had the honor of throwing out the first ball—an honor never before given an active player. And, of course, he met with Kuhn many times during the season as The Hammer charted his course in baseball history.

Henry Aaron, now 40, is older, wiser and more articulate today than when he broke in as a quiet, skinny, scared rookie scarcely 20 years old. He makes an excellent character study.

His lines about the nature of hitting are worth thinking about. He once said, "Guessing what the pitcher will throw is eighty per cent of being a successful hitter. The other twenty per cent is just execution. All real good hitters guess a lot. You're a dumb hitter if you don't guess some."

And, on another occasion, when he was in the midst of a 22-game batting streak, he said, "I don't worry about hitting streaks. You either do or you don't where those are concerned."

Henry Aaron is always serious on the diamond. "I never smile when I have a bat in my hands," he concedes. "That's when you've **got** to be serious. When I get out on the field, nothing's a joke to me. I don't feel I should walk around with a smile on my face."

He is a quiet man who leads by example on the field but generally keeps to himself. "I'm basically a private person," he says. "I've always been that way. I've always been a loner and despite the publicity, I'm still the same."

Hank has many friends and values his relationships with them as much as they value their relationships with him. One close friend is Joe Walker, sports director of radio station WXAP in Atlanta. "I just love him," says Walker of Aaron. "We go way back to Jacksonville when he first broke in. I call him Henry Everywhere, not Henry Aaron. It goes back to when he was a second baseman in one game and fielded everything in sight."

His friends helped him get through the difficult time following his divorce, and are helping him now that the pressure is at its peak in the race with Ruth.

Though he prefers not to discuss the divorce, he did tell a Newsweek reporter, "My divorce was really something to go through, especially with four kids involved. I think I threw myself into baseball to get my mind off it, but there were still periods when I was really depressed. It took a long time to get back on the right track."

Another subject he likes to play down is his contract, a three-year agreement signed on Feb. 29, 1972. The pact calls for an estimated $200,000 per season.

He explains: "I wanted a three-year contract mainly because I didn't want any distractions in the last stages of the chase. Business arguments can get you all confused and I don't want that."

The only distractions Aaron has now are the constant stream of interviewers who not only monopolize his time at the ballpark, but who also follow him to his Atlanta apartment. An enterprising press crew even found him fishing in Mobile Bay on one occasion.

"Everyone is human and there may be a time when Hank will just want to hide," says Eddie Mathews. "When he was turned away by the 'all-white' hotels years ago, he had to find his own lodgings. He made many good friends and they'll be eager to help him. If he gets a few days off, you can be sure that the news media will never find him."

In addition to his numerous activities and obligations off the field, Aaron is a member of the President's Council on Physical Fitness and was also named the representative from the sports world on the list of the ten best-dressed men in the U.S. by the Custom Tailors Guild of America. He's played in the American Airlines golf classic in Puerto Rico, an event which precedes the opening of baseball training camps in February.

He's a quiet man, a thinker, and a strategist. He knows who he is, what he wants, and where he is going. And, after he gets there, he will leave one of his loves—baseball—for another, his family. When he makes that move, he will do it because he feels it is the right decision to make.

"Baseball is the only thing I have ever known. I just want to go out with good health and fond memories." •

Aaron (L) and Dave Johnson are congratulated by Commissioner Kuhn for 1973 heroics.

Since 1971, Hank Aaron has symbolized baseball's biggest weapon—the home run.

DOWN MEMORY LANE

■ Hank Aaron's name appears first in the 1974 edition of "Who's Who in Baseball" just as it has every year for the past 20. The man has played a long time and piled up many baseball records. His achievements will linger in the minds of his contemporaries on the field and in the thoughts of millions of fans who had the privilege of seeing him play. And, after retirement, Henry Aaron himself will look back on a career that is one of the finest in the game's annals.

The commotion caused by the Aaron-Ruth race has created a new image for Hank Aaron—that of a home run hitter. Prior to 1971, when he reached a personal peak with 47 home runs, he had been regarded as a good all-around player, a man who could hit for both average and power, and could also run, throw, and field. Even he considered himself that type of player. Then things changed.

"When I hit forty-seven home runs in 1971," he says, "I began to think I could break Babe Ruth's record.

"I started to swing more consciously for homers in 1972 than ever before in my career. The fact is that I have a chance to equal or surpass perhaps the most respected record on the baseball books. I'd be foolish not to do everything I could to accomplish the feat."

Aaron is still a good all-around player—as his .301 average, 96 RBI, and good work in the field showed in 1973—but his name has become synonymous with the supreme feat of the baseball batsman: the home run. The fact that Hank and homer both start with the same letter made it just that much easier for the nation's headline writers to get that image across.

When the Hammer gets the homer that cracks Ruth's record—he refers to it as THE home run—it will certainly be one of his most cherished moments. The tying home run too will prove to be a significant moment in his illustrious career. But Hank has had many other important home runs, including No. 700, a shot he delivered in July 1973 off Philadelphia (now Pittsburgh) southpaw Ken Brett.

At the moment, the No. 1 spot on his personal list is occupied by the pennant-winning homer Hank clouted off Billy Muffett of the St. Louis Cardinals on Sept. 23, 1957. The 11th-inning blow came with teammate Johnny Logan on second and the Braves locked in a 2-2 game with the Cards at Milwaukee County Stadium. It enabled the team to represent the Western city in the World Series for the first time and participate in its first post-season activity since 1948, when the Braves were still in Boston. Aaron's homer had "pennant" written all over it. The ball disappeared deep over the fence in dead centerfield, more than 402 feet from home plate.

In his very next at-bat, the budding super-star slammed another home run of personal significance. That blow, which came in the first inning of the next day's game against the Cardinals, not only represented the first grand-slam of Aaron's career, but also gave the 23-year-outfielder the first of four N.L. home run titles he has won. The victim was a pretty fair pitcher: Sam (Toothpick) Jones, a righthander who later enjoyed a 21-win season for the Giants.

Aaron continued his hot hitting in the World Series against the Yankees, with a .393 average and three homers. But he doesn't list any of those clouts on his list of personal favorites. "The Yankees came back to tie us after every home run I hit," he explains, "so I can't rate any of them on my list since none of them won a ball game."

The 1957 season was a big one for Aaron because the Braves not only won the World Series, but he also won the National League's Most Valuable Player Award in a close contest with Stan Musial of St. Louis. Henry edged the Cardinal star in balloting, 239-230.

Another mid-1950s homer that The Hammer remembers is the first of his career, hit April 23, 1954 off Vic Raschi, the one-time Yankee great who was then winding up his career with the St. Louis Cardinals. The homer came in the seventh major-league game of Aaron's career, which promised to be

Aaron belted No. 500 off Mike McCormick of Giants on July 14, 1968.

a good one. But no one knew just how **good**.

"We knew he had a tremendous amount of talent, we knew he could play, we knew he could hit, but that's about all we knew," says Eddie Mathews, recalling his impressions of Aaron at that time.

That first home run ranks at the head of a list of milestone Aaron homers which includes No. 500, a shot he belted off lefthander Mike McCormick of the Giants on July 14, 1968 at Atlanta. After that game, Aaron told reporters, "This equals the thrill of hitting the home run that won the 1957 pennant in Milwaukee."

"I remember touching each base right in the center," he continued. "I knew it was gone when I hit it. I'd been trying to hit it for a few days when I came to bat for the last time in a game. I'm glad it came in a victory because I wanted it to mean something, and I'm glad it came off McCormick because he was the Cy Young Award winner last year and is an outstanding pitcher."

The Hammer was also glad to deliver No. 500 in front of the Braves' fans, especially since all his previous milestone shots had come on the road. "I wanted to hit it in front of the fans who have been so good to me and the Braves," said Aaron, who got No. 500 in front of 34,826 fans who gave him a lengthy standing ovation after the clout. "I got a tremendous thrill from their reaction."

There was a mild disappointment in the timing of the historic event, however. Aaron's father, hoping to witness it, had just left town after staying in Atlanta three days. There was a week-long interval between No. 499 and No. 500, prompting Henry to tell Braves' chief executive Bill Bartholomay, "I'm sorry you had to wait so long," as the slugger passed Bartholomay's box on the way to the dugout.

No. 600 was also delivered against a tough San Francisco pitcher, this time a righthander, Gaylord Perry. Aaron had hit only one home run off Perry—in 1964—prior to belting No. 600 on April 27, 1971.

Since the Braves did not win the game in which The Hammer reached the 600 mark—a level achieved before only by Babe Ruth and Willie Mays—that blast is not listed among his 10 most memorable home runs. Yet, it was a watershed mark in the slugger's great career because it was the blow that generated—for the first time—serious talk that Aaron could break Babe Ruth's career record.

After the game, Aaron was asked about the legendary mark. "It's a long way off," he said. "I'll just try to get one home run at a time. I'm not really a home run hitter. I like to think of myself as a complete ballplayer. I'd like to be remembered as a good all-around player, not just as a fellow who hit home runs."

Perry, the victim of No. 600, had taunted Aaron before the game, saying, "If he gets it off me, he'll have to earn it." Aaron met the challenge by hitting the ball squarely and hitting it a long way when he connected in the third inning with one man on base.

"I guessed fastball and I got it," said Aaron later. "Perry tried to jam me but missed by about two inches and I got a clean shot at it. I knew it was gone the minute I hit it."

Perry was also the pitcher who gave up Aaron's dramatic All-Star home run in Atlanta on July 25, 1972. With the American League nursing a 1-0 lead in the sixth and Perry, who was to win the Cy Young Award in his first year with Cleveland, on the hill, Aaron came to bat. The tension mounted as 53,107 fans hoped their idol could come through.

The righthander with the out-of-sight sinker (many experts call it a spitball) delivered a pitch just off the plate and Aaron zipped a line drive over the left-centerfield fence to put the Nationals ahead temporarily, 2-1, and drive the fans slightly bananas.

That home run, Aaron has said several times, remains the most dramatic of the 752 home runs he has hit as a professional player (Ruth had 731 all told). "I was flying," Aaron told a crowd of newsmen in the victorious NL clubhouse after the 1972 All-Star contest. "It was a great feeling."

Aaron might have been the game's MVP if spray-hitting Cookie Rojas hadn't turned into an instant strongman to put the AL ahead again, 3-2, with a two-run homer later on. The press box had already voted Aaron the MVP, figuring his homer had been the game-winner, but a second vote was taken after Joe Morgan singled home the winning run in the 10th to give the Nationals a 4-3 decision. Morgan topped Aaron in the second vote.

The Atlanta All-Star homer was the second in two All-Star Games for Aaron, who had connected with a Vida Blue serve the previous year in Detroit. Oddly, in 19 previous All-Star appearances, this supreme power-hitter had not hit a ball out of the park and had, in fact, failed to hit even a double or a triple.

The All-Star slump did not detract from The Hammer's regular-season clouting, however. His most explosive display came on June 21, 1959, when he powered home runs off three different pitchers in a single game at San Francisco's Seals Stadium, used by the Giants before the move to Candlestick Park the following season.

The victims of Aaron's assault, which almost included a fourth home run,

Gaylord Perry taunted Aaron before giving up No. 600 to Hank.

old Connie Mack Stadium on April 20, he yielded Henry Aaron's 400th home run.

It was a milestone because it was the number of homers Hank had set as his career goal back in 1954, when he was a rookie in the spring camp of the Milwaukee Braves. But, the star adds with a laugh, "I didn't know it was my 400th until after the game."

Another Philly pitcher, righthander Ray Culp, gave up Hank's last Milwaukee homer on Sept. 20, 1965. That blow closed out a hectic era of major league ball in Wisconsin and ended the first half of Henry Aaron's uphill race toward baseball immortality . . . although he could hardly have guessed it at that time.

"We played just two more games in County Stadium after that," Aaron remembers. "Then it was on to Atlanta."

Once he arrived in Atlanta, Hank Aaron became an instant home run hitter. He began to pull the ball for the first time, rather than trying to hit to all fields. The new strategy worked immediately, as he tied the record for most home runs through June 30 with 24. No. 24 came off righthander Larry Jackson, then with Philadelphia. It capped the

were Johnny Antonelli, a lefthander, and Gordon Jones and Stu Miller, two righthanders. All three homers were two-run blasts.

"Seals Stadium was a great park for righthanded hitters," Aaron remembers.

Young lefthanded pitchers on their way down are also good for righthanded hitters. Bo Belinsky, who pitched a no-hitter as a rookie with the 1962 California Angels, was such a southpaw with the 1966 Philadelphia Phillies. In the ninth inning of a game at hottest home run streak in Aaron's career.

One rap against Aaron in his race with Ruth is that he doesn't hit homers for distance, as the Babe did. Yet, this charge is far from the truth. While Ruth collected many "easy" homers because of the short right-field porches at both the Polo Grounds and Yankee Stadium, Aaron always had to hit his home park home runs at least 320 feet in Milwaukee and 330 in Atlanta.

Often, he hit the ball much further. He and Earl Williams are the only men ever to reach the upper deck at Atlanta Stadium, for example.

The longest Aaron homer probably was the blast he hit on June 18, 1962 at the Polo Grounds, then the home of the fledgling New York Mets. This blast was no pot-shot down the rightfield line—far from it. It was a titanic blast to the deepest part of the ancient ballyard—deep in the centerfield bleachers.

The previous night, Lou Brock, then with the Cubs, had hit a ball into the centerfield bleachers, a spot reached only once before—by Milwaukee's Joe Adcock, who turned the trick against the Giants before they moved to San Francisco.

When the Braves came to town, writers rushed Aaron and popped the question, "Did you hear about Brock's shot?"

The Hammer responded, "Where did it go?"

A newsman volunteered, "See that seat about five rows back in the bleachers? Just against the stars leading to the clubhouse? It was unbelievable. No one will ever do it again. They're tearing the place down after next year."

With the bases loaded in the third inning, Aaron teed off on the first pitch from Jay Hook, an off-season mathematician who could explain the inner secrets of the curve ball but couldn't throw a good one. The ball landed slightly to the left of where Brock's had gone the night before.

Aaron's reaction after the game? "I just wanted to see if it could be done," he said.

Just three days earlier, Aaron had hit his last home run—also a grand-slam—against Pittsburgh's 42-year-old rookie, Diomedes Olivo. Back-to-back grand slams? If anyone could do it, Henry Aaron seemed like the most logical candidate. In 1962, he had a typical year: 45 homers, 128 runs batted in, and a .323 average.

"A lot of players live on last year if it's a good one," says

"Every time you go to the plate is a new time," says homer king Hank Aaron.

Aaron, who always tries to improve on his over-all performance. "I try to look ahead to the next season. I don't want one good year and then a bad one. One of the things I'm proudest of is my consistency. Every day is a new day and everytime you go to the plate is a new time. That last time up is like yesterday's newspaper—it's gone."

But Aaron never worried about his batting average. "That's something for the men with the pencils to worry about," he once said. "I'll hit as many as I can and you guys figure out what it comes to."

Henry Aaron has played in nearly two-dozen All-Star Games, two World Series, one NL best-of-three playoff, and one NL best-of-five championship series. He's led the league in batting twice and in homers and RBIs four times each. The fact that he's never won the coveted Triple Crown—emblematic of leadership in all three categories in the same season—is a tribute to his steady performance. He never dominated the league like a Ralph Kiner or Willie Mays, but always was at or near the top in every offensive category.

His list of memories is long. He remembers teaming with Eddie Mathews, Joe Adcock, and Frank Thomas to slug consecutive home runs in a single inning at Cincinnati on June 8, 1961—the first time that feat had ever been accomplished. He remembers playing against the long-retired Vic Raschi, Stan Musial, Don Drysdale, and many others. And he remembers his fans, who gave him special "nights" on Aug. 23, 1968 and again on May 26, 1970, when The Hammer was honored for his 3,000th hit and the Braves' Hoyt Wilhelm was feted simultaneously for appearing in his 1,000th game as a pitcher, an all-time record.

As a hitter, Aaron has patterned himself after Joe DiMaggio, the famed Yankee Clipper. "He was the symbol of cool perfection," Aaron recalls. "He was the type who, to me, did everything right. This symbolizes a great ballplayer."

Asked to name the best players he has played with or against, Hank came up with this team:

Catcher—Del Crandall
First base—Willie McCovey
Second base—Jackie Robinson
Shortstop—Bobby Wine
Third base—Eddie Mathews or Clete Boyer
Outfield—Willie Mays
Outfield—Roberto Clemente
Pitchers—Warren Spahn, Sandy Koufax, Don Drysdale, Juan Marichal, Bob Gibson, Tom Seaver
Manager—Walter Alston

"If I needed one man to do one job—hitting, fielding, running bases or stealing them, I'd have to pick Mays," said Aaron several years ago, before Mays started his sharp decline in all departments.

Of his second base choice, Robinson, Aaron says, "He was my idol. He gave every black kid in America something to look forward to. He was intelligent, went about his business, and took all the pressure. People talk about pressure on me, but it's nothing compared to what Jackie went through."

Aaron has much to say about the great pitching he's faced through the years. "For me, Curt Simmons was the toughest," he said, "but Koufax was always tough too. He threw a great fastball and a great curve ball. It's not unusual for a righthander to have trouble with lefties," continued Aaron, noting that both Simmons and Koufax threw from the port side. "If you're a good pitcher, you're a good pitcher. It doesn't really make much difference whether you're right or lefthanded.

"You know, even with Koufax, some lefthanders gave him as much trouble as righthanders. I remember when Stan Musial was playing, he probably hit Warren Spahn (a lefty) as hard as anybody, and he was a lefthanded hitter. It's just what the pitcher throws up there to you.

"Sam Jones, Don Drysdale,

Don Drysdale is one of the pitchers on Aaron's personal all-time team.

Don Newcombe . . . all these guys were really great pitchers and very tough for me," he went on. "Of course, Tom Seaver, Bob Gibson, and people like that have given me plenty of trouble too. I can't remember having any great days against pitchers like Gibson, but I'm sure I've hit a few home runs off them and, of course, they've gotten me out quite a few times."

One thing sticks out in Hank's memory. "The constant adjustment to the pitching is the toughest thing for me," says Aaron, who has made five hits in a game three times and four hits in one contest 45 times.

The batting figures don't show it, but Aaron does have trouble with a pitcher on occasion. Generally, he does make the necessary adjustments and spoils the confidence of the pitcher, who thinks he has found a secret way to silence Aaron's bat. The truth is there really is no way to pitch him. "Just keep the ball away," says one senior NL hurler, "and hope."

There will be more memories for Hank Aaron's mental library after the 1974 season ends. They are sure to include the two biggest home runs of his career . . . the two that will make Henry Aaron the new king of swat. •

WHAT DOES THE FUTURE HOLD?

■ On the night Henry Aaron hit his 600th career home run, Willie Mays listened to the Atlanta Stadium fans give their hero a long and lusty ovation, then said, "He's not through rocking this place yet. If you think the fans got shook up tonight, tell 'em to just stick around."

Since that April evening in 1971, Henry Louis Aaron has done just that. In the 1974 season, Henry Aaron's bat will deliver the biggest jolt of all.

"When No. 715 sails off his bat, Hank officially becomes the greatest home run hitter in baseball history," says Eddie Mathews. "It makes you tingle just to think about it. You just know Hank will make the big one a beauty and you can only imagine the size of the ovation he will get as he trots around the bases—the man who topped Babe Ruth. I'd just like to be the first one to shake his hand."

Contrary to some ill-founded rumors, Aaron won't quit after topping the 715 mark with his second home run of the season. "I'll play the full season," he promises. "I signed a three-year contract two years ago and I fully intend to honor that contract."

To prepare for his final campaign on the active list, Aaron watched his weight during the winter months and turned down the vast majority of requests that he appear at various award banquets. "I'll make four or five," he said at the start of the hot stove league season in mid-October. "Those things only put weight on you and I'm too old to have to take it off during spring training."

The Atlanta super-star knows he will break the coveted record set by Ruth between 1915 and 1935. And he feels he has the support of most American sports fans.

Aaron looks into the future—and sees a full season with Braves in 1974.

"I get letters chastising me for trying to break Ruth's record," he concedes, "and that's to be expected. But for every letter I get against setting the record, I get four or five for it. Nowadays, I think most people want to see all records erased. It shows a progression in sports, an attitude that we can do better now than athletes did in the past."

Most of the National League's veteran umpires are pulling for Aaron. "I'd love to be behind the plate when Hank Aaron hits the home run that will put him one up on the great Babe Ruth," says Ed Sudol.

"If you want to know if we feel any special pressure, the answer is no," notes Billy Williams. "We're up there calling balls and strikes for every player in every game."

Donald Davidson adds: "When Roger Maris was going for Ruth's single-season record, he had a time limit and pressure from day to day. This is not the case with Aaron. Everyone knows that sooner or later he will hit 715 home runs and many more."

Aaron, who hopes to close out his career with a fine all-around season, says, "I just want to hit the ball hard every time. I've found the home runs will come when you don't go after them. I know the pitchers will work me carefully and I've just got to discipline myself to wait for nothing but good pitches."

The Hammer already holds the major league record for most intentional walks and is certain to add to it before the 1974 season ends. Eddie Mathews says even walks to Aaron that aren't obviously "intentional" should be listed in that category.

"Some walks aren't listed as intentional," says the manager, "but they're actually very intentional. The other team decides it will throw Hank nothing worth hitting. If he wants to swing, that's his business."

Aaron's knowledge of the strike zone and of the flight path of different pitches is so good that umpires sometimes seem reluctant to call a pitch a strike if Aaron doesn't swing at it. It is no surprise that Henry, despite being a perennial slugger, ranked only fifth in career strikeouts among active players in 1973—behind Harmon Killebrew, Willie Mays, Frank Howard, and Frank Robinson.

Opposing pitchers, naturally, are aware of the slugger's sharp eye, excellent perception, and uncanny ability to do things with a bat in his hands. The man who served up Babe Ruth's 714th and last homer, Guy Bush, offers his version of the proper way to pitch to Aaron: "If I was pitching and Aaron came up to bat, I'd dust him off. Anything to get him out of the game."

Other hurlers might disagree; Aaron, always cool under tension or pressure, might just rebound to hit a home run on the next pitch.

The slugging flyhawk doesn't always hit home runs—or even singles, for that matter. His .301 batting average in 1973 meant he was successfully retired by the opposing pitcher in virtually seven of every 10 at-bats. This ratio helped The Hammer make up his mind against the designated-hitter rule initiated by the American League—but not the National—in 1973.

"If I strike out with the bases loaded and two men out," says Aaron, "I want to be able to pick up my glove and try to redeem myself with a big play in the field."

Under the DH rule, a man is designated to bat in place of the pitcher whenever the pitcher's batting turn comes up. The pitcher is allowed to remain in the game. The DH, of course, is simply a substitute batsman who does not play defense.

If the National League had adopted the rule, it is conceivable that Aaron, conserving his strength for four or five swings a game, might have passed Babe Ruth in career home runs in 1973. But the slugger didn't like the idea because he felt it might advance the argument of the pro-Ruth crowd that Aaron broke the record unfairly.

"They're going to say that irregardless," comments Eddie Mathews. "A lot of people are happy about it and some people are unhappy. All I know is he has played an awfully long time and he's certainly earned the right to break the record."

After the record-breaking home run becomes baseball history sometime in April 1974, the Braves plan to fete their super-star with a special tribute at Atlanta Stadium.

"We're going to have a real nice night for him after he breaks the record," says Bob Hope, director of public relations and promotions for the team. "Anything we thought about doing prior to that event wouldn't be adequate because we're going to have to celebrate properly afterwards."

Already, there's a recording called "Move Over Babe," originally written by Detroit Tigers broadcaster

Ernie Harwell and recorded by pitcher Bill Slayback of the Toledo Mud Hens, a Tiger farm club. When the disc was released nationally on the Carla label, it was recorded by Richard (Popcorn) Wiley. It's a catchy tune and was quickly picked up and played by pop stations all over the country.

Locally, the Atlanta Chamber of Commerce is promoting a massive program called "Atlanta Salutes Hank Aaron," to include billboards, a college scholarship drive, a home run countdown board at the Atlanta airport, production of special artwork and tapes for local television and radio stations, and the naming of special memorials to Aaron, including a street, a school, and possibly even a statue.

"We set out to accomplish three goals," explained Bradley Currey Jr., president of the Chamber. "We wanted to commemorate Hank's actual breaking of the record, to honor Hank in a perpetuating manner, and finally, to let the world know how proud Atlantans are of Hank Aaron."

Once he gets by the excitement and fanfare involved in the actual record-breaking and the acclaim it will bring, Aaron will probably turn his attention,

Aaron predicts great things for Dusty Baker (above) and Darrell Evans.

once again, to helping the younger players on the Braves. He cares deeply about the team's future after he leaves.

Of his current teammates, he feels Darrell Evans and Dusty Baker may someday remind fans of the famous combination of Eddie Mathews and Hank Aaron. There are many similarities. Evans and Mathews were both white, lefthanded, power-hitting third basemen who improved once-sloppy defense play through hard work. Baker is a young, black, all-around player who can hit for average and for power, run extremely well, and field his position.

"I've always been a Darrell Evans booster," Aaron says. "Pretty soon, I'll retire and the Braves can count on having someone capable of hitting 35 home runs a year for a long time to come. He's a patient hitter and that's especially important in a power hitter. The publicity I'm getting now and the lack of it for him may be a blessing in disguise. There's no pressure on him at all right now and nobody is expecting him to do great things just yet.

"As for Dusty Baker, I think he's one of the fine young players in the game today and has the ability to become a super-star."

Evans hit 41 homers and knocked in 104 runs in 1973 to win the attention of writers and broadcasters who named him the best third baseman in the majors in a special poll for The Associated Press. Baker, who had hit .321 in his first full season in 1972, hit .288 with 22 home runs and 99 RBI in 1973 and fielded magnif-icently. But Dusty had a tough assignment—he had to follow Henry Aaron in the Braves' batting order.

"It's been tough to hit behind Hank," Baker con-ceded after the 1973 season closed. "Sometimes after he hits a home run, you hear the crowd, and then there's a sudden hush. You have to wait for the crowd to die down because, after all, they came to see Hank.

"The other night was a first for me," continued the 24-year-old outfielder. "There were about 10,000 people in the stadium, we were behind by a couple of runs in the eighth inning, and as soon as Hank hit, everybody left. The other guys said to me, 'Hey, Dusty, what'd you do to the crowd?'

"It's just a little different than last year or in previous years. Hank always had somebody a little more established hitting behind him, like Orlando Cepeda or Rico Carty. In the past, it was me watching those guys and now it's me in the same position that they were in.

"It's toughest after he hits a home run because you have to wait a few minutes. You don't have to wait **too** long!"

Though Aaron tries to coach or advise younger players from time to time, he admits they don't always listen. "They have their own ideas about things," he says. "You start talking to a younger player today telling him how to play and I find myself listening to him, shaking my head 'yes.' They're tough to talk to— young kids today—they have their own ideas about everything."

One of the most little-known facts about the Aaron-Ruth race is about an old man rather than a young player. He's 86-year-old George E. (Duffy) Lewis, probably the only man besides Ruth to witness The Babe's first and last home runs. Lewis was the only man ever to pinch-hit for Babe Ruth and, ironically, he was also the first man to give Hank Aaron his major league meal money. Lewis was traveling secretary of the Milwaukee Braves when Aaron arrived in 1954.

Aaron himself would like a front-office job when he's through as a player. "I've got five cases full of trophies and awards and they haven't gotten me anything yet," he says somewhat bitterly. "I don't want nobody holding no charitable funds for me, holding days for me, or passing out hats. I think my ballclub should reward me the same kind of way Stan Musial was rewarded when he retired."

Musial became an executive with the Cardinals after his retirement in 1963. Eleven years later, Hank Aaron is hoping for the same consideration and recognition.

"While the Braves' future plans for their super-slugger remain unknown, Hank will have a busy off-the-field life under the auspices of the William Morris Agency and its subsidiary, W.M.A. Sports, Inc.

"Hank will be the home run king for a long, long time and as the king he will be the toast of the world," explains Berle Adams, president of W.M.A. Sports. "We are planning a personal appearance tour and commercially-profitable tie-ins with Japan, Mexico, and other baseball countries in Latin America. Hank will retain his title for many years and will be a major figure in public life during all that time."

The Hammer might even consider transferring his talents to the silver screen. "It depends on what part I'd have to play," he says. "Let me just say that I'm a baseball player and I've never played in any type of movie before, although I'm not afraid of a new challenge. I know there would probably be a lot of homework I would have to do. But I've always said I can't play baseball forever and I have to go on making a living."

Berle Adams says: "If Henry is asked to do a motion picture as an actor, it will probably be with a director who is a real baseball fan himself. They'll treat him very carefully and make sure he comes off well. Most of the people in show business are fans and the right director can do a lot with anybody."

Aaron's show business career officially began with appearances on a number of TV talk shows and a lengthy "roasting" on the Flip Wilson Show shortly before Thanksgiving. Of course, he had appeared in a number of commercials previously, especially for Wheaties and Oh Henry candy bars. More ads are in the offing.

"We will not allow him to endorse or work with a product that isn't top-notch," Adams explains. "We won't take any questionable product and ask him to endorse it. It would be harmful to him, to baseball, and to us."

For the moment, Aaron is concentrating on one goal—having a strong 1974 season that may help put the Braves into the World Series. He gets support for that objective in many ways, but especially in inspiring mail from young fans. "I hope you catch up with Baby Root," read one letter. "You are my idol," read another. "You always were and you always will be. I hope you get traded to the New York Mets." A

third read, "I remember you when I bit into an Oh Henry candy bar. I hope you beat that other guy in homers."

Rationing his time for interviews may be a problem, but he coped with it well in 1973. "What I need," said The Hammer, "is a computer to feed these questions into and see what the answers are."

Jim Fanning, one-time Braves' executive who is now general manager of the Montreal Expos, explains the significance of Aaron's race with destiny. "It will be," he says, "the most exciting moment in sports history when Hank ties and then passes Babe Ruth."

Of all the players who have come and gone in the history of major league baseball, few were more deserving of the home run crown than Henry Louis Aaron, a humble man with exceptional skills and a fierce ambition beneath a calm exterior.

"Hank turned out to be, in my opinion, one of the finest ballplayers who ever lived," says Lew Burdette, a former Braves' pitcher and coach. "Maybe he didn't have the flair of a Mays or a Clemente, but when the dust cleared, he was always standing on the same base that they were on."

Only he got there first. ●

A COMPARISON

George Herman Ruth (The Babe)

b. Feb. 6, 1895, Baltimore, Md.
d. Aug. 16, 1948, N.Y., N.Y.

6-2, 235 pounds

Batted and threw left

Played 22 seasons in majors

Entire career under 154-game schedule

Never played night ball

Began as star pitcher, gradually became full-time outfielder

Signed by Boston Red Sox, traded to Yankees in 1920, released in 1935 and signed by Boston Braves

Faced 7 opposing clubs throughout career

Furthest club from New York was St. Louis; team traveled strictly by train

Relief pitching a rarity

No TV; radio play-by-play began in 1930's, near end of career

No pressure; set own new record several times

White star faced no prejudice

Aimed at cozy dimensions of 254 feet in Polo Grounds and 296 at Yankee Stadium in right field

Advantage of being lefty, facing mostly right-handed pitching

SUMMATION: Might have hit more HRs if in better physical condition or if he had been outfielder from the beginning of his career

---

Henry Louis Aaron (The Hammer)

b. Feb. 5, 1934, Mobile, Ala.

6-0, 180 pounds

Bats and throws right

Entered 21st season in 1974 with pledge to retire after season

Broke in under 154-game schedule in 1954, began playing current 162-game schedule following first expansion in 1962

Plays majority of games at night

Signed as infielder, arrived in majors as outfielder

Signed with Boston Braves, played for Milwaukee Braves and moved with club to Atlanta

Faced 7 opposing pitching staffs when he broke in, then 9 starting in 1962, and 11 starting in 1969

Coast-to-coast travel began in 1958; jet-lag became factor in playing career

Emphasis on relief specialists

Faces constant exposure in mass media

Pressure of challenging another man's record

Hate mail because he is black

Home runs had to travel 320 ft. in Milwaukee and 330 ft. in Atlanta to clear fences

Disadvantage of being righthanded, facing mostly righthanded pitching

SUMMATION: Might have hit more HRs if not playing night games, facing pressures of racial tensions and Ruth's legend, and enduring time-zone changes caused by travel

---

Night games, air travel are factors in Hank Aaron's home run totals.

HENRY LOUIS (HANK) AARON

Born February 5, 1934, at Mobile, Ala.
Height, 6.00. Weight, 180.
Bats and throws righthanded.

BATTING RECORD
Italic face figures indicate led league or tied for league lead.

Year	Club	P	G	AB	R	H	TB	2B	3B	HR	RBI	Pct.
1952	Eau Claire	SS	87	345	79	116	170	19	4	9	61	.336
1953	Jacksonville	2B	137	574	*115*	*208*	*338*	*36*	14	22	*125*	*.362*
1954	Milwaukee	OF	122	468	58	131	209	27	6	13	69	.280
1955	Milwaukee	OF-2B	153	602	105	189	325	*37*	9	27	106	.314
1956	Milwaukee	OF	153	609	106	*200*	*340*	*34*	14	26	92	.328
1957	Milwaukee	OF	151	615	*118*	198	*369*	27	6	*44*	*132*	.322
1958	Milwaukee	OF	153	601	109	196	328	34	4	30	95	.326
1959	Milwaukee	OF-3B	154	629	116	*223*	*400*	46	7	39	123	*.355*
1960	Milwaukee	OF-2B	153	590	102	172	*334*	20	11	40	*126*	.292
1961	Milwaukee	OF-3B	155	603	115	197	*358*	*39*	10	34	120	.327
1962	Milwaukee	OF-1B	156	592	127	191	366	28	6	45	128	.323
1963	Milwaukee	OF	161	631	*121*	201	*370*	29	4	*44*	*130*	.319
1964	Milwaukee	OF-2B	145	570	103	187	293	30	2	24	95	.328
1965	Milwaukee	OF	150	570	109	181	319	*40*	1	32	89	.318
1966	Atlanta	OF-2B	158	603	117	168	325	23	1	*44*	*127*	.279
1967	Atlanta	OF-2B	155	600	*113*	184	*344*	37	3	*39*	109	.307
1968	Atlanta	OF-1B	160	606	84	174	302	33	4	29	86	.287
1969	Atlanta	OF-1B	147	547	100	164	*332*	30	3	44	97	.300
1970	Atlanta	OF-1B	150	516	103	154	296	26	1	38	118	.298
1971	Atlanta	1B-OF	139	495	95	162	331	22	3	47	118	.327
1972	Atlanta	1B-OF	129	449	75	119	231	10	0	34	77	.265
1973	Atlanta	OF	120	392	84	118	252	12	1	40	96	.301

Major League Totals . . . . . 2964 11288 2060 3509 6424 584 96 713 2133 .310

WORLD SERIES RECORD

		G	AB	R	H	TB	2B	3B	HR	RBI	Pct.
1957	Milwaukee vs New York	7	28	5	11	22	0	1	3	7	.393
1958	Milwaukee vs New York	7	27	3	9	11	2	0	0	2	.333
	World Series Totals	14	55	8	20	33	2	1	3	9	.364

CHAMPIONSHIP SERIES RECORD

		G	AB	R	H	TB	2B	3B	HR	RBI	Pct.
1969	Atlanta vs New York	3	14	3	5	16	2	0	3	7	.357

ALL-STAR GAME RECORD

		AB	R	H	TB	SB	2B	3B	HR	RBI	Pct.
1955 at Milwaukee	rf	2	1	2	2	0	0	0	1	0	1.000
1956 at Washington	lf	1	0	0	0	0	0	0	0	0	.000
1957 at St. Louis	rf	4	0	1	1	0	0	0	0	0	.250
1958 at Baltimore	rf	2	0	0	0	0	0	0	1	0	.000
1959 at Pittsburgh	rf	4	1	2	0	0	0	0	1	0	.500
1959 at Los Angeles	rf	3	0	0	0	0	0	0	1	0	.000
1960 at Kansas City	rf	4	0	0	0	0	0	0	0	0	.000
1960 at New York (American)	rf	3	0	0	0	0	0	0	0	0	.000
1961 at San Francisco	ph	1	1	1	1	0	0	0	0	0	1.000
1961 at Boston	rf	2	0	0	0	0	0	0	0	0	.000
1962 at Chicago (National)	cf	2	0	0	0	0	0	0	0	0	.000
1963 at Cleveland	rf	4	1	0	0	0	0	0	0	0	.000
1964 at New York (National)	ph	1	0	0	0	0	0	0	0	0	.000
1965 at Minnesota	rf	5	0	1	1	0	0	0	0	0	.200
1966 at St. Louis	lf	4	0	0	0	0	0	0	0	0	.000
1967 at California	cf-lf	6	0	1	1	0	0	0	0	1	.167
1968 at Houston	rf	3	0	1	1	0	0	0	0	1	.333
1969 at Washington	rf	4	1	1	1	0	0	0	0	0	.250
1970 at Cincinnati	rf	2	0	0	0	0	0	0	0	0	.000
1971 at Detroit	rf	2	1	1	4	0	0	1	1	0	.500
1972 at Atlanta	rf	3	1	1	4	0	0	1	2	0	.333
1973 at Kansas City	lb	2	0	1	1	0	0	0	1	0	.500
All-Star Totals 21 Games		64	7	13	17	0	0	2	8	2	.203

HANK AARON'S
━━ MILESTONE HOME RUNS ━━

No.   1—April 23, 1954, at St. Louis, off Vic Raschi

No. 100—August 15, 1957, at Cincinnati, off Don Gross

No. 200—July 3, 1960, at St. Louis, off Ronnie Kline

No. 300—April 19, 1963, at New York, off Roger Craig

No. 400—April 20, 1966, at Philadelphia, off Bo Belinsky

No. 500—July 14, 1968, at Atlanta, off Mike McCormick (S.F.)

No. 600—April 27, 1971, at Atlanta, off Gaylord Perry (S.F.)

No. 700—July 21, 1973, at Atlanta, off Ken Brett (Phila.)

No. 713—September 29, 1973, at Atlanta,
        off Jerry Reuss (Hou.)

GEORGE HERMAN (BABE) RUTH

WORLD SERIES RECORD

Year	Club	Pos.	G	AB	R	H	2B	3B	HR	RBI	BA	PO	A	E	FA
1915—Boston		PH	1	1	0	0	0	0	0	0	.000	0	0	0	.000
1916—Boston		P	1	5	0	0	0	0	0	1	.000	2	4	0	1.000
1918—Boston		P-OF	3	5	0	1	0	1	0	2	.200	1	5	0	1.000
1921—New York		OF	6	16	3	5	0	0	1	4	.313	9	0	0	1.000
1922—New York		OF	5	17	1	2	1	0	0	1	.118	9	0	0	1.000
1923—New York		O-1B	6	19	8	7	1	1	3	3	.368	17	0	1	.944
1926—New York		OF	7	20	6	6	0	0	4	5	.300	8	2	0	1.000
1927—New York		OF	4	15	4	6	0	0	2	7	.400	10	0	0	1.000
1928—New York		OF	4	16	9	10	3	0	3	4	.625	9	1	0	1.000
1932—New York		OF	4	15	6	5	0	0	2	6	.333	8	0	1	.889
World Series Totals			41	129	37	42	5	2	15	33	.326	73	12	2	.977

PITCHING RECORD

Year	Club	G	IP	W	L	Pct	H	R	ER	SO	BB	ERA
1914—Balt.-Prov.		35	245	22	9	.710	219	88	..	139	101	..
1914—Boston		4	23	2	1	.667	21	12	10	3	7	3.91
1915—Boston		32	218	18	8	.692	166	80	59	112	85	2.44
1916—Boston		44	324	23	12	.657	230	83	63	170	118	1.75
1917—Boston		41	326	24	13	.649	244	93	73	128	108	2.02
1918—Boston		20	166	13	7	.650	125	51	41	40	49	2.22
1919—Boston		17	133	9	5	.643	148	59	44	30	58	2.97
1920—New York		1	4	1	0	1.000	3	4	2	0	2	4.50
1921—New York		2	9	2	0	1.000	14	10	9	2	9	9.00
1930—New York		1	9	1	0	1.000	11	3	3	3	2	3.00
1933—New York		1	9	1	0	1.000	12	5	5	0	3	5.00
Totals		163	1221	94	46	.671	974	400	309	488	441	2.28

WORLD SERIES RECORD

Year	Club	G	IP	W	L	Pct	H	R	ER	SO	BB	ERA
1916—Boston		1	14	1	0	1.000	6	1	1	4	3	0.64
1918—Boston		2	17	2	0	1.000	13	2	2	4	7	1.06
World Series Totals		3	31	3	0	1.000	19	3	3	8	10	0.87

The great Babe Ruth hit 15 home runs in World Series competition.

Author Dan Schlossberg with Hank Aaron in 1969.

ABOUT THE AUTHOR

DAN SCHLOSSBERG is a freelance baseball writer who has been an admirer of the Braves in general and Hank Aaron in particular since the salad days of the late 1950s. Since Dan follows no other professional sport, he devotes his total attention to baseball all year round and has become an authority on the game and the men who play it. He has a comprehensive personal baseball library, a fine memory, and valuable contacts both in the game and in sports press boxes. The former Associated Press Sports Editor for New Jersey, Dan is now a regular contributor to a wide range of publications, including the paperback book Baseball Stars of 1974, and such magazines as Baseball Digest, Baseball Illustrated 1974, Sports Quarterly Baseball, All-Star Sports and Super Sports, among others. He holds B.A. degrees in both journalism and political science from Syracuse University (1969) and lives in Passaic, N.J.